It's Elementary
Schoolhouse-Inspired Quilts for Home and School
By Kim Gaddy

It's Elementary

Schoolhouse-Inspired Quilts for Home and School

By Kim Gaddy

Editor: Judy Pearlstein
Designer: Kelly Ludwig
Photography: Aaron T. Leimkuehler
Illustration: Eric Sears
Technical Editor: Deanna Hodson
Photo Editor: Jo Ann Groves

Published by:
Kansas City Star Books
1729 Grand Blvd.
Kansas City, Missouri, USA 64108

Kansas City Star Quilts moves quickly to publicize corrections to our books. You can find corrections at www.KansasCityStarQuilts.com, then click on "Corrections."

First edition, first printing
ISBN: 978-1-61169-139-9

Library of Congress Control Number: 2014944993

Printed in the United States of America by Walsworth Publishing Co., Marceline, Missouri.

To order bulk copies, call StarInfo at (816) 234-4473; to order single copies, call (816) 234-4242.

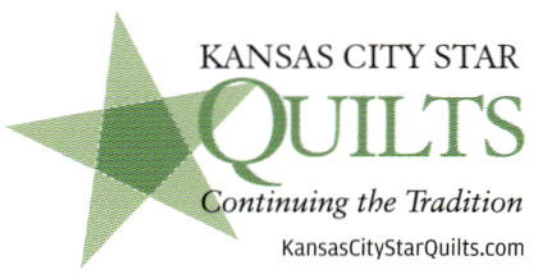

About the Author

Kim Gaddy lives in Pflugerville, Texas, with her husband and two feisty terriers. Now that her kids are grown and out of the house, Kim divides her time between her pattern design business (Buttons and Bees) and her new career as an acute care nurse.

Table of Contents

Introduction

I've always loved school. In fact, I love school so much I'm going back to school myself. In between my nursing studies I've been working on this book and thinking about projects that may appeal to students of all ages.

A great deal of thanks goes out to my mom, Becky Magness, who taught me to sew. She designed and sewed the charming Pinwheel quilt on page 30. And thank you to Osie Lebowitz, from needleandthread.com, for her quilting on the quilts in this book.

Once again, it's been a pleasure to work with Judy Pearlstein from Kansas City Star Quilts. Thanks for all your patience as I've struggled to sew and study.

Kim Gaddy

Applique Instructions

All the applique in this book was done using fusible webbing and a zigzag stitch. It's about as easy as applique can get, and it will hold up to the wear and tear better than many other methods.

Use the instructions on the fusible webbing of your choice to cut out your applique shapes and fuse them to the background fabric.

Stabilize the background fabric with lightweight fusible interfacing or stabilizer marketed for embroidery. Using thread that matches the applique shape in both the top spool and bottom bobbin, zigzag around each applique shape. I set the stitch width to about ⅛" or narrower, and set the stitches about as tight as I would for sewing a buttonhole. If you're new to this technique and have a ½ speed on your sewing machine, set your machine to slow so you can zigzag around curves more smoothly.

Happy Sewing!

— Schoolhouse Quilt —

Quilt measures 60" x 70"

Cutting guidelines for schoolhouse blocks

(21 blocks total)

Red fabrics

- A – 1 ½" x 3" rectangles, cut 42
- C – 4 ½" x 1 ½ " rectangles, cut 21
- D – 1 ¾" x 2" rectangles, cut 42
- F – 3" squares, cut 21
- H – 1 ¼" x 1 ½" rectangles, cut 42
- K – 6" x 1 ½" rectangles, cut 42
- M – 1 ¼" x 3" rectangles, cut 42
- O – 1 ½" x 3" rectangles, cut 21

Ivory fabrics

- B – 2 ½" x 3" rectangles, cut 21
- E – 2" squares, cut 21
- F – 3" squares, cut 21
- G – 2 ½" x 1 ½" rectangles, cut 42
- I – 5" x 1 ½" rectangles, cut 21
- J – 6 ½" x 3" rectangles, cut 21
- L – 1" x 5" rectangles, cut 21
- N – 2" x 3" rectangles, cut 42
- P – 10 ½" x 1 ½" rectangles, cut 42

Black fabric

Using the template on p. 70, cut 21 roof pieces. Cut five 2" strips, then sub-cut into 21 – 2" x 7 ¼" roof units.

Material

- 1 ⅜ – 1 ⅞ yards of red fabrics
- 8 yards of ¼" wide red single fold bias tape
- ⅜ – ⅝ yard black fabrics for roof applique
- 3 ½ – 4 yards ivory fabric
- 1 ¼ - 1 ¾ yards gray fabrics
- ⅝ yard fabric for binding
- Fusible webbing (optional)
- Batting, 64" x 74"
- Backing 3 ½ yards of 44" wide

Note: If you are going to have your quilt quilted by a long arm quilter, you may need extra fabric and batting. Check with your quilter for backing requirements.

Cutting guidelines for chain blocks

(21 blocks total)

Gray fabrics

- Q – 4 ½" squares, cut 21
- R – 2" squares, cut 168

Ivory fabrics

- S – 7 ½" x 2" rectangles, cut 84
- T – 4 ½" x 2" rectangles, cut 84

Backing

Cut fabric into two 1 ¾ yard pieces, and sew together along the 1 ¾ yard side.

If you are going to have your quilt quilted by a long arm quilter, you may need extra fabric. Check with your quilter for backing requirements.

Schoolhouse Block Instructions

All seam allowances are ¼" wide. Sew right sides together.

Sew a piece A to either side of piece B (house door) along the 3" side. Press.

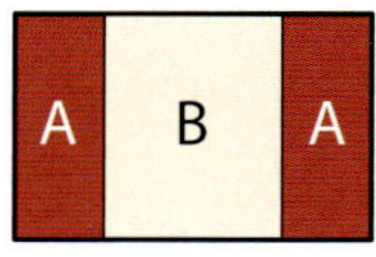

Sew piece C to the top of the house door unit in the pervious step.

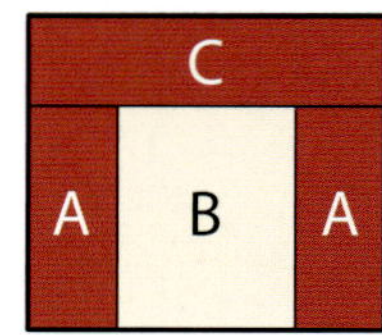

Applique a single ¼ strip of bias tape down the center of each ivory square E (over door window).

Sew a piece D to each side of square E. Press.

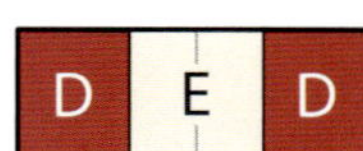

Sew the over door window unit to the door unit.

Sew 21 - 2" (finished size) half-square triangles. Using a fabric pen or pencil, draw a diagonal line across the back side of each ivory square, piece F. Right sides together, match each of the 21 red squares, piece F, to an ivory square. Sew a seam on either side of the marked line using a ¼" seam allowance. Cut along the marked line. Press seams open. Trim squares to 2 ½".

Sew the half-square triangle units together into groups of two. Match the red sides and sew down that line. See graphic for guidance.

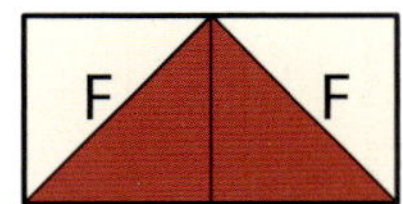

Sew the half-square triangle unit to the top of the window unit.

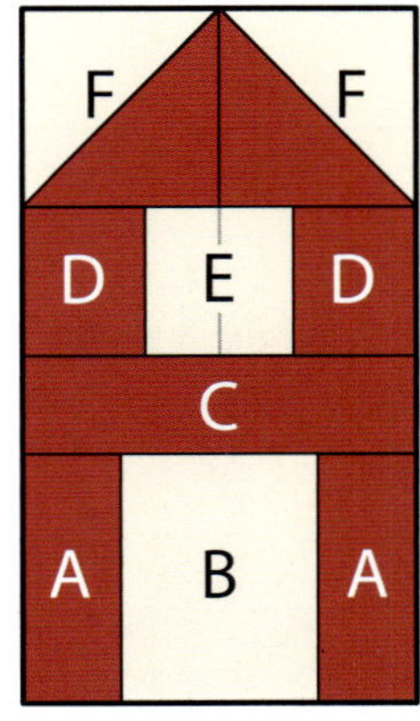

On each of the windows, piece N, applique a strip of bias tape down the middle in each direction to make a windowpane design.

Sew one piece M to one side of each window, piece N. Join the two windows by sewing piece O in between the window units. Press seams.

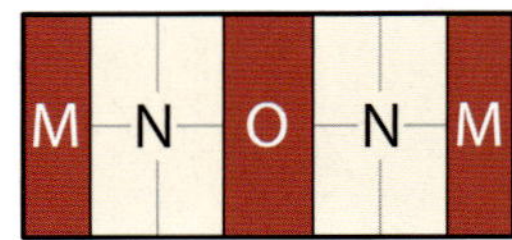

Sew a piece K to the top and bottom of the window unit. Press.

Sew ivory piece L to one side of the window unit. Press.

With the ivory piece L faced to the left, sew ivory piece J to the top of the window unit. Press.

Sew this window unit to the door unit.

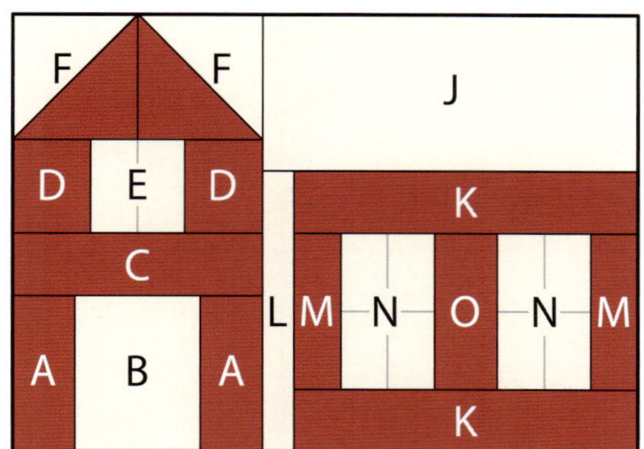

Construct the roof unit by sewing an ivory piece G to one side of each chimney piece H. Press. Join each of these units with an ivory piece I. Join a chimney piece to either end of piece I.

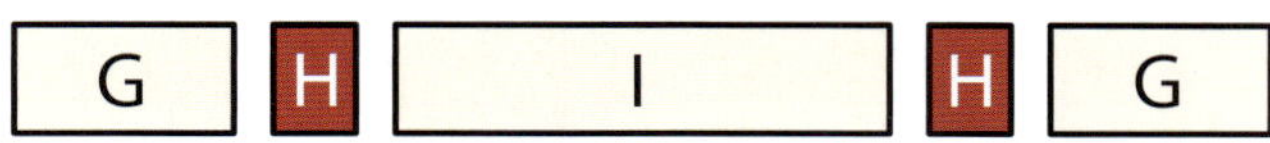

Join the roof unit to the top of the house unit.

To square up the block, sew a piece P to the top and bottom of the house.

Applique the roof to the block. (The template is on p. 70.) Use fusible webbing or the method of your choice.

Trim block to 10 ½" square.

Chain Block Instructions

All seam allowances are ¼" wide. Sew right sides together.

Sew an ivory piece T to opposite sides of each 4 ½" gray square, piece Q. Press.

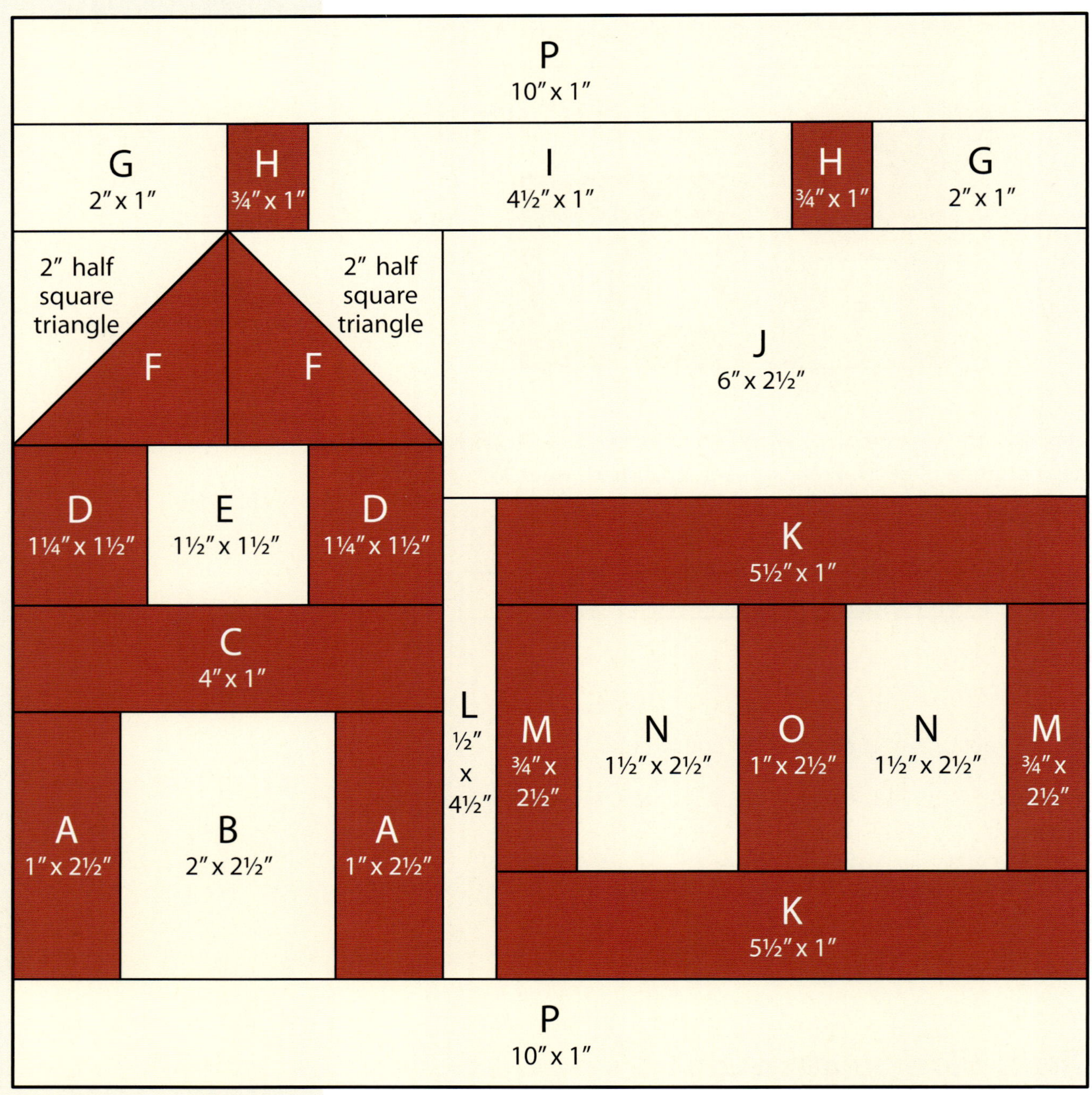

These measurements do not include seam allowances.

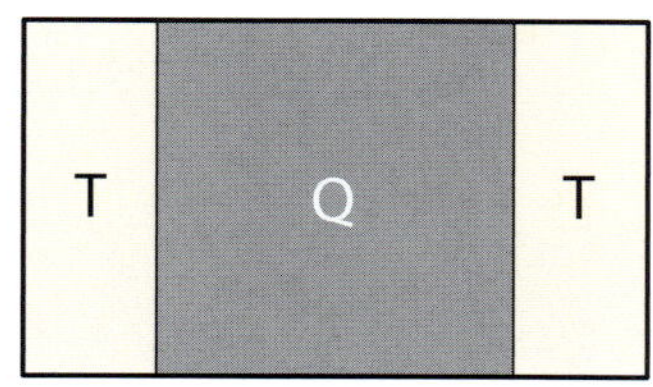

For the remaining 42 ivory rectangles, piece T's; sew a gray square R to each end. Press.

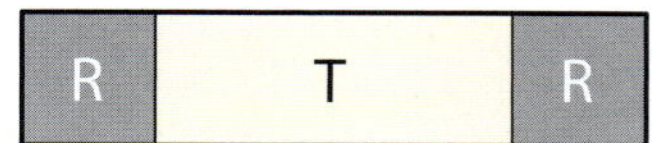

Sew the R/T units to opposite sides of the T/Q units.

Sew an ivory piece S to opposite sides of the previous unit. Press.

For the remaining 42 ivory rectangles, pieces S, sew a gray square R to each end. Press.

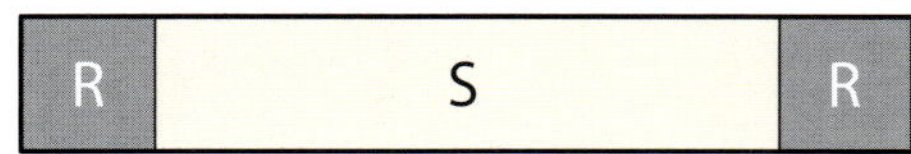

Sew these R/S units to opposite sides of the previous block. Press.

Trim block to 10 ½" square.

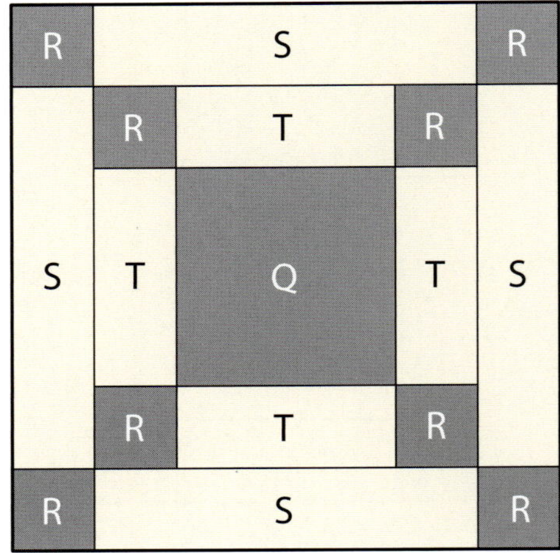

Construct Quilt

Sew together seven rows of six blocks (alternating schoolhouse and the chain blocks), and then join the rows together. Press. Square up quilt top.

Quilt as desired.

— Kids —

Quilt measures 47 ½" x 60 ¾"

Don't let the wonky "eighths of an inch" measurements fool you. *This quilt is simple to construct. Just pay attention to your ruler markings and you'll be fine. Plus if you use the strip piecing method to piece the children, this quilt goes together quicker than you'd think. This quilt would make a great gift for a special teacher. To personalize the quilt, you could have the children write their names on their own block like an album quilt.*

Material

- ¼ yard in each of two greens, two yellows, two oranges, two reds, one pink, one purple, one turquoise, denim blue, dark blue, black and gray for the children's clothing
- ¼ yard in each of beige, tan and brown for the children's skin
- 3 ½ yards of ivory for the background
- ½ yard fabric for binding
- Batting, 52" x 64"
- Backing, 55 ½" x 69 ¾"

Note: If you are going to have your quilt quilted by a long arm quilter, you may need extra fabric. Check with your quilter for backing requirements.

Cutting guidelines for girl blocks

(66 blocks total)

Piece A – Cut 66 from various colors of clothing fabric for the dress. (The template is on page 70.)

Piece B – Cut 66 B1s and 66 B2s (from the strip you will piece using strips E and F below).

Strip C – Cut one 1 ½" strip along the width of your fabric (45" wide), out of tan, beige and brown fabric. These will become your girls' heads.

Strip D – Cut 12 – 1 ¾" strips of ivory fabric. These will be pieced to either side of the girls' heads and legs.

Strip E – Cut two ⅞" strips each along the width of your fabric out of tan, beige and brown. These are the girls' arms. You will have six strips total. This is one part of the arm unit from which you will cut pattern pieces B1 and B2.

Strip F – Cut six 2 ⅜" strips along the width of your fabric out of ivory background fabric. This is the other part of the arm unit from which you will cut pattern piece B1 and B2.

Strip G – Cut two ⅞" strips along the width of your fabric out of tan, beige and brown fabrics. These will become the girls' legs.

Strip H – Cut three ¾" strips along the width of your ivory background fabric. These strips will go between the girl's legs.

Cutting guidelines for boy blocks

(66 blocks total)

Strip C – Cut one 1 ½" strip along the width of your fabric (45" wide), out of tan, beige and brown fabric. These will become your boys' heads.

Strip D – Cut six 1 ¾" strips of ivory fabric. These will be pieced to either side of the boys' heads.

Strip J – Cut four 1 ¼" x 11" strips each of fabric out of tan, beige and brown fabrics. These will become the boy's arms.

Strip K – Cut one 2 ½" x 11" strip of fabric for the boys' sleeves out of green, turquoise, gray, red, orange and yellow. You should have six strips total.

Strip L – Cut one 1 ⅞" x 22" strip out of each of the six colors you used for strip K. These are the boy's shirts.

Strip M – Cut two ¾" x 22" strips each out of denim blue, dark blue and black fabric. These are the pants waistbands.

Strip N – Cut two 1" x 22" strips each out of denim blue, dark blue and black fabric. These are the pants legs.

Strip O – Cut six ¾" x 22" strips out of ivory background fabric. This strip will go between the pants legs fabric.

Strip P – Cut 11 1 ⅝" strips along the width of your ivory background fabric. Sub-cut the strips into 132 – 3 ⅜" strips. This strip will be pieced on either side of the boy's bodies.

Cutting guidelines for sashing

Cut 31 – 1 ¼" strips along the width of your ivory background fabric for the sashing strips. You can cut as you sew.

These measurements are FINISHED sizes.
See pattern instructions for cut sizes.
Each block measures 3½"x 4¼" finished size.

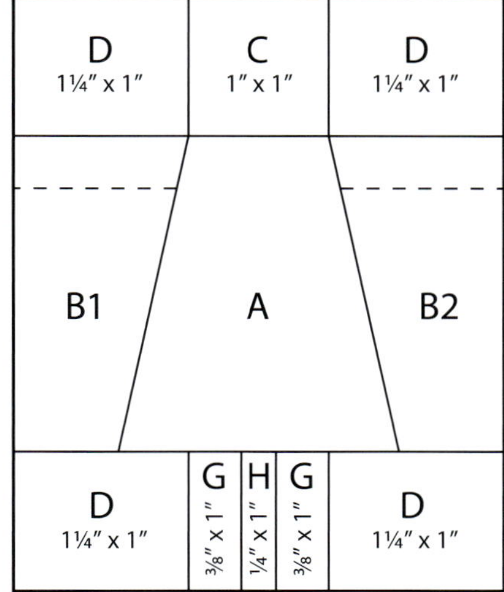

D 1¼" x 1" | C 1" x 1" | D 1¼" x 1"

J ¾" x ⅜" | K 2" x ⅜" | J ¾" x ⅜"

P 1⅛" x 2 ⅞" | L 1¼" x 1⅜" | M 1¼" x ¼" | N ½" x 1¼" | O ¼" x 1¼" | N ½" x 1¼" | P 1⅛" x 2 ⅞"

Girl Block Instructions

The diagram does not include seam allowances. All seam allowances are ¼" wide. Sew right sides together.

Working head to toe:

Head. Sew a strip D (ivory background) on either side of each strip C (tan, beige, or brown flesh color). Press seam towards the flesh color. Cut these strips into 1½" wide units. You should have 66 total head units that measure 4" x 1 ½". *Note: This will be repeated for the boys heads.*

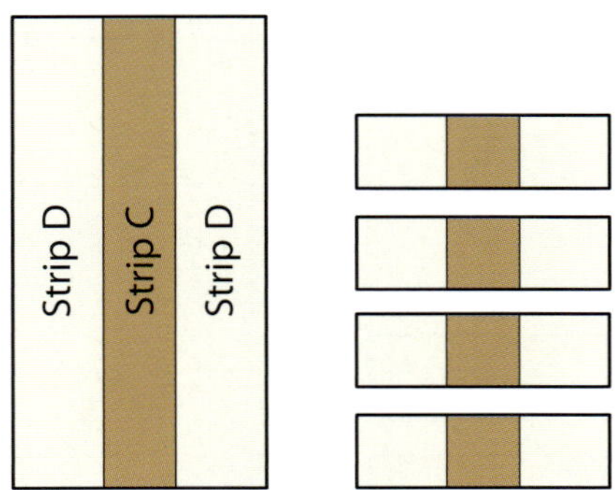

Arms. Sew each strip E (tan, beige or brown flesh color) to each strip F (ivory background). Press seams open. Cut 11 B1 and 11 B2 pieces from each of the tan, beige and brown pieced strips. *Note: the B1 and B2 pieces must be positioned on the pieced strip so that the arm fabric is at the top of the pattern piece when cut. Use the diagram below as a cutting lay-out guide.*

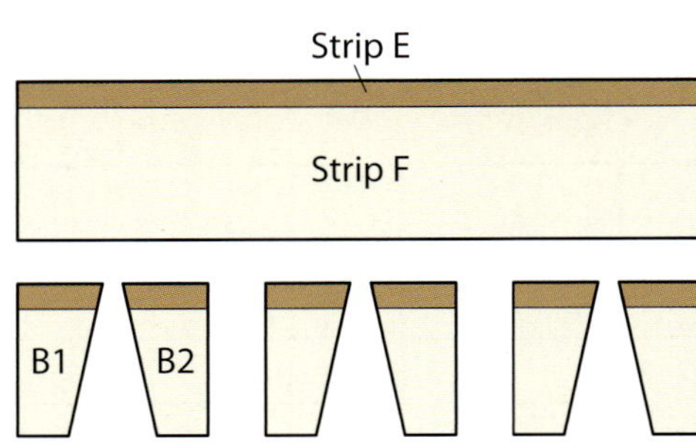

Dress. Sew a B1 and a B2 arm unit to either side of each A piece (girl's dress). Press seam toward dress. The dress units should measure 4" x 2 ¾".

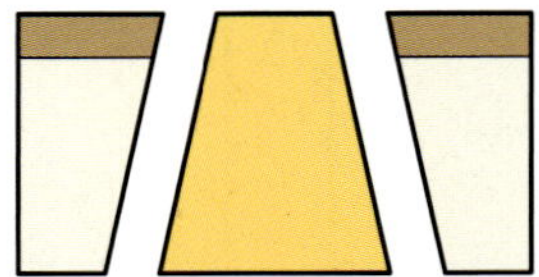

Legs. Piece together one wide strip by sewing together narrower strips in the following order: D-G-H-G-D. See below. Press seams open. Cut the wider strip into widths of 1 ½". Leg units should measure 4" x 1 ½". You should have 22 leg units for each flesh color (66 total).

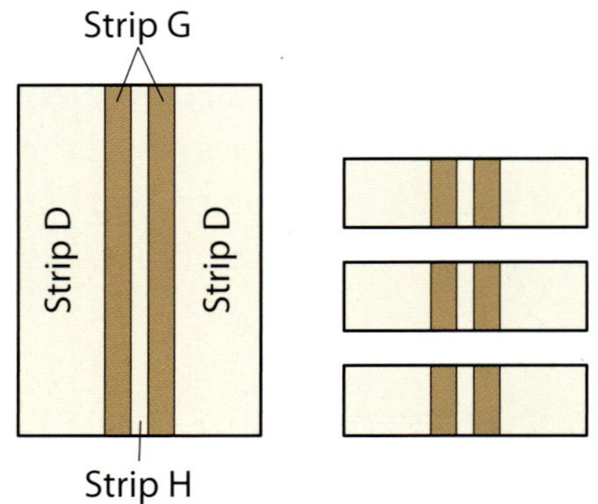

Complete the block. Matching flesh colors, sew a head unit to a dress unit. Press seams open. Matching flesh colors, sew a dress unit to a leg unit. Press seam towards the dress.

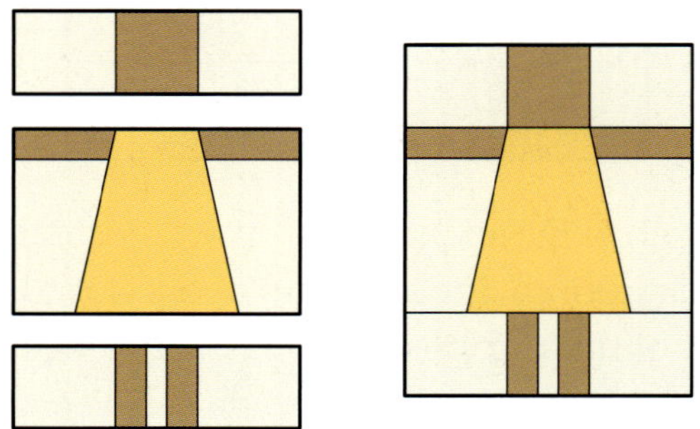

Trim blocks to 4" x 4 ¾". Finished size is 3 ½" x 4 ¼".

Boy Block Instructions

All seam allowances are ¼" wide. Sew right sides together.

Head. Sew a strip D (ivory background) on either side of each strip C (tan, beige, or brown flesh color) as you did for the girls' heads. Press seam towards the flesh color. Cut these strips into 1½" wide units. You should have 66 total head units that measure 4" x 1 ½".

Arms and sleeves. Sew a strip J (tan, beige or brown) on either side of strip K (shirt sleeve fabric). Just make sure that the strip K gets two strip Js of the same fabric so arm color matches. Cut this strip into ⅞" wide units that measure 4" x ⅞" (66 total sleeve units).

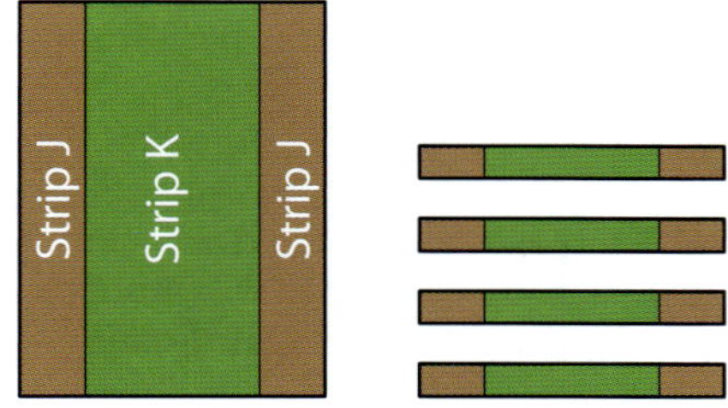

Shirt and waistband. Sew a strip M (waistband) to each strip L (shirt). Press seam open. Cut this strip into 1 ¾" wide units that measure 2 ⅛" x 1 ¾" (66 total shirt units).

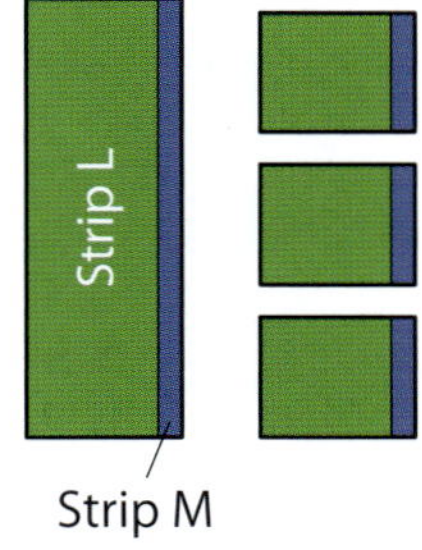

Pants legs. Piece together one wider strip by sewing together narrower strips in the following order: N-O-N. See below. Press seams open. Cut the wider strip into 1 ¾" wide units that measure 1 ¾" square (66 total pants leg units).

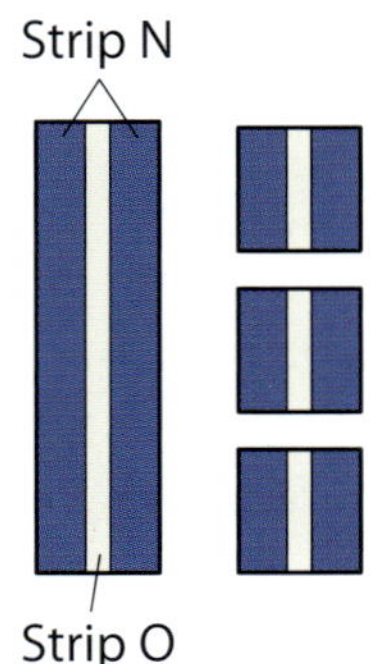

Complete the block. Matching flesh colors, sew each head unit to a sleeve unit. Press seams open. Sew each shirt unit to a pants leg unit. Sew a strip P (ivory background fabric) to either side of the shirt + pants leg units. Press seams towards ivory fabric. This new unit should measure 4" x 3 ⅜". Matching shirt colors, sew each head/sleeves unit to a shirt/pants unit. Press seams open. Trim block to 4" x 4 ¾".

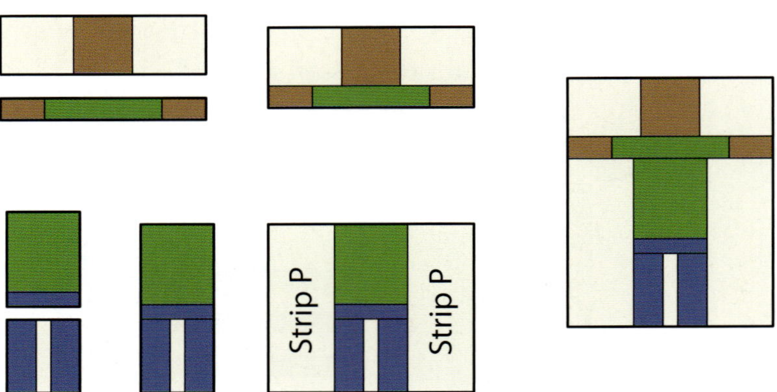

Piece the quilt

Sew 12 rows of boys and girls (using 11 boys and girls to make a row). Use 1 ¼" wide (cut size) sashing to join boys and girls to form rows. You can cut as you sew or sub-cut WOF sashing strips into 144 – 4 ¾" pieces for piecing between the boy and girl blocks and on the end of each row. Measure your blocks before cutting. Press seams towards the sashing.

Sew the remaining strips together and sub-cut into 13 – 47 ½" sashing strips to add between the rows and on the top and the bottom of the quilt. Again, measure your rows before cutting. Then join rows of boys and girls with the 1 ¼" wide sashing.

The quilt top should measure approximately 48" x 61 ¼". Quilt as desired.

Crayola
Crayola

— Crayons and Pencils Quilt —

Quilt measures 45″ x 76"

Cute and colorful, this quilt is sure to brighten up any classroom or bedroom. *Use primary colors like the quilt pictured or modify the colors to match your décor.*

Cutting guidelines for crayon blocks

(40 blocks total)

Templates are on p. 71.

Piece A, crayon point – Cut 5 purple, 5 orange, 5 red, 5 green, 4 turquoise, 4 dark gray, 4 blue, 4 brown, 4 pink

Piece B, background – Cut eight – 4" strips WOF (width of fabric). Sub-cut into 40 each of templates B1 and B2

Piece C, crayon piece – Cut at 2" x 3 ½" – 5 purple, 5 orange, 5 red, 5 green, 4 turquoise, 4 dark gray, 4 blue, 4 brown, 4 pink.

Piece D, crayon paper wrap – Cut at 3 ½" x 12 ¾" – 5 light purple, 5 light orange, 5 light red, 5 light green, 4 light turquoise, 4 gray, 4 light blue, 4 light brown, 4 light pink.

Piece E, crayon bottom – Cut at 2 ¼" x 3 ½" – 5 purple, 5 orange, 5 red, 5 green, 4 turquoise, 4 dark gray, 4 blue, 4 brown, 4 pink.

Cutting guidelines for bias tape

Cut 560 inches of ⅝" strips (14 – ⅝" strips across the width of your fabric) from the black fabric to make ¼" bias tape strips to embellish the crayons.

Material

- ¼ yard each of purple, orange, turquoise, dark gray, red, blue, brown, green and pink fabric for crayons
- ⅓ yard each light purple, light orange, light turquoise, light gray, light red, light blue, light brown, light green and light pink fabric for crayon paper wrappers
- ⅝ yard yellow fabric for pencils
- ¼ yard light brown fabric for pencils
- ⅛ yard lead black fabric for pencils
- ⅛ yard gray for pencils
- ¼ yard pink for pencil erasers
- ¼ yard light gray for markers
- 10" x 4" scraps of fabric for marker tops and bottoms in light green, green, blue, two reds and orange
- 1 yard of ivory background fabric
- ½ yard black fabric to make scant ¼" bias tape for crayon detail
- Batting, 49" x 80"
- Backing, 2 ¼ yards, 54" wide, or piece together 2 ¼ yards of 45" wide fabric

Note: If you are going to have your quilt quilted by a long arm quilter, you may need extra fabric. Check with your quilter for backing requirements.

Cutting guidelines for pencils

(14 blocks total)

Templates are on page 72.

Pencil wood strip – Cut two 2 ¼ " wide light brown strips across the width of the fabric.

Pencil lead strip – Cut two 1 ¾" wide lead gray strips across the width of the fabric.

Piece F, pencil point – (The strips above will be combined for creating Piece F in the pencil instructions on p 27.)

Piece G – background – Cut two 4" strips WOF, sub-cut into 14 each of pieces G1 and G2 from ivory background fabric. (The templates are on page 72.)

Piece H, pencil – Cut five 3 ½" strips WOF, sub-cut into 14 – 12 ¼" pieces from yellow fabric.

Piece J, pencil metal ferule – Cut a 2 ¼" strip WOF, sub-cut into 14 – 3 ½" pieces from gray fabric.

Piece K, pencil eraser – Cut 14 – 3 ¼" x 3 ½" units from pink fabric.

Cutting guidelines for markers

(6 blocks total)

Piece L - Cut six – 1 ¾" x 3 ½" units from ivory background fabric.

Piece M, marker top – Cut one each at 3 ½" x 7 ½" from light green, green, blue, 2 reds and orange fabric.

Piece N, marker body – Cut six – 3 ½" x 10 ½" from light gray.

Piece O, marker bottom – Cut one each at 1 ¼" x 2 ½" from light green, green, blue, 2 reds and orange fabric.

Piece P – Cut 12 – 1" x 1 ¼" from ivory background fabric.

Crayon Block Instructions

(40 blocks total):

All seam allowances are ¼" wide. Sew right sides together.

Crayon point. Sew a piece B on either side of each piece A. Press seam away from the ivory fabric.

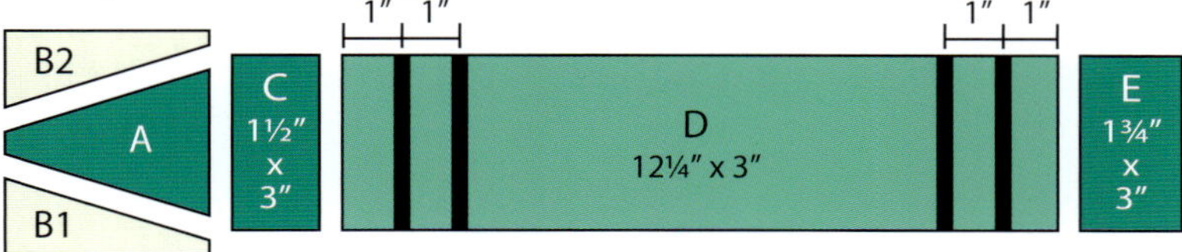

Diagram does not include seam allowances.

Use the guide to piece the rest of the crayon. Crayons measure 19 ½" x 3 ½".

Applique two rows of black bias tape to each end of the crayon paper wrapping. Place the first black stripe, one inch inside the paper wrapper. Place the second strip one inch inside the first.

Pencil Block Instructions

(14 blocks total):

All seam allowances are ¼" wide. Sew right sides together.

Piece together each 2 ¼" wide light brown strip with a 1 ¾" wide lead gray strip. Press the seam open. Cut 14 F pieces from this strip. The template is on p. 72.

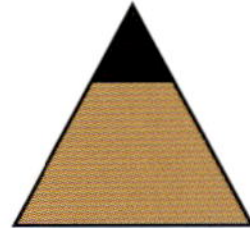

Pencil point. Sew a piece G on either side of each piece F. Press the seam away from the ivory fabric.

Use the diagram to piece the rest of the pencil. Pencils measure 19 ½" x 3 ½".

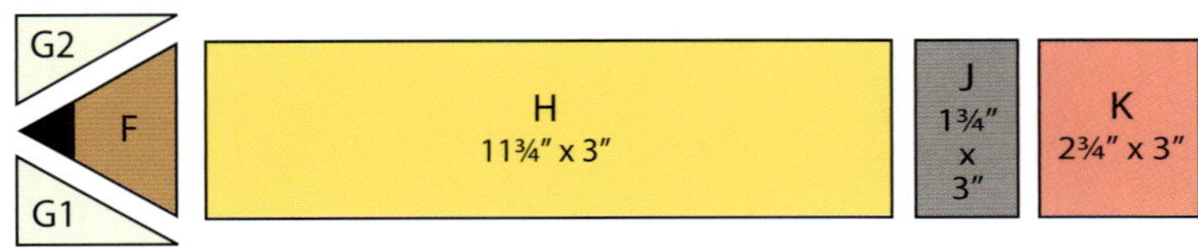

Diagram does not include seam allowances.

Marker Block Instructions

(6 blocks total):

All seam allowances are ¼" wide. Sew right sides together.

Marker bottom. Sew a piece P to each side of piece O. Press the seam open.

Marker. Use the guide to piece the rest of the marker. Markers measure 19 1/2" x 3 1/2".

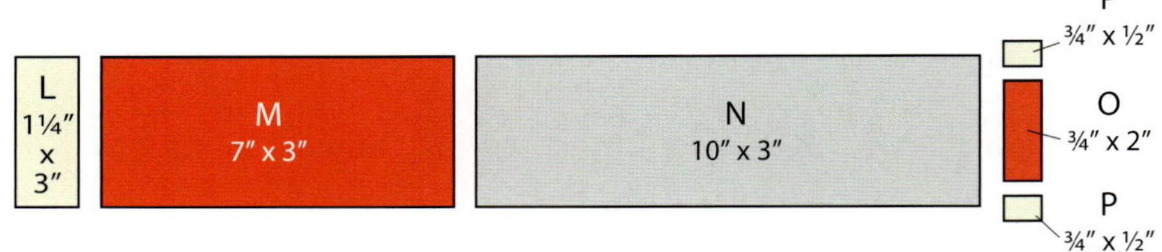

Diagram does not include seam allowances.

Piece the quilt

Use the photo on page 29 to lay out your blocks. Piece four rows of 15 writing tools. Join the rows to complete the quilt top. The quilt top should measure approximately 45 ¼" x 76 ½". Quilt as desired.

Rainbows and Pinwheels —Nap Quilt—

Designed and pieced by Becky Magness

45" x 54"

Cutting

- 3 ⅛" squares, 60 white
- 3 ⅛" squares, 60 black

*To make the quilt as shown in the picture, use 12 medium blue, 6 light blue, 12 yellow, 27 green, 21 red and 12 orange squares.

Pinwheel Block Instructions

All seam allowances are ¼" wide. Sew right sides together.

Using a fabric pencil or marker, mark a diagonal line across the wrong side of each of the sixty 3 ⅛" white squares.

Right sides together (RST) match each white square with a black square.

With a ¼" seam allowance, sew a seam on either side of the marked line. Cut the triangles apart on the marked line.

Press the seams toward the black fabric. You should now have 120 half-square triangle units measuring 2 ¾" square.

Sew together four half-square triangle units to form each pinwheel block below. You should have 30 pinwheel blocks measuring 5" square.

Material

- Two charm packs, or 90 – 5" squares*
- ½ yard white
- ½ yard black
- ½ yard fabric for binding
- Batting, 49" x 59"
- Backing, 1 ¾ yards, 54" wide, or piece together 2 ¾ yards of 45" wide fabric

If you are going to have your quilt quilted by a long arm quilter, you may need extra fabric. Check with your quilter for backing requirements.

Rainbow Block Instructions

Each rainbow block consists of one pinwheel block and three 5" squares of fabric.

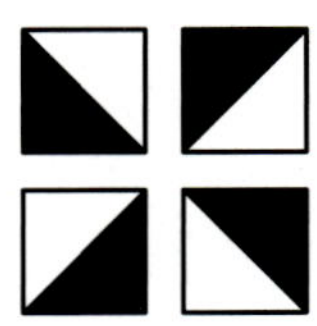

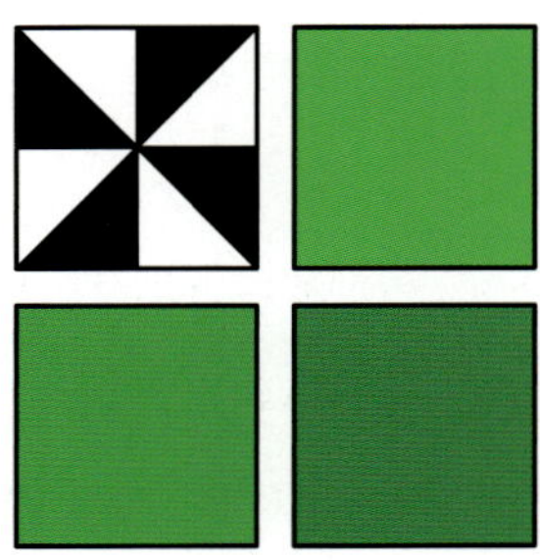

You should have 30 rainbow blocks measuring 9 ½" square.

Construct the quilt

Follow the quilt diagram to lay out your rainbow blocks or design your own arrangement.

Sew five blocks together into rows, and then sew six rows together to complete the quilt top.

Press. Layer the quilt top, batting and backing. Baste, and then quilt as desired.

— Reading Pillow —

Finished size: 17 ½" x 12"

Cutting Instructions

Applique templates are on pp. 73 – 77. Use a narrow zigzag stitch to create the mice tails.

Constructing the pillow

Using the fusible webbing technique found on page 5, cut out applique shapes and arrange on pillow front and back. Fuse in place. Also fuse light interfacing or stabilizer to the wrong side of pillow front and back.

Using thread that matches the applique shapes and a tight narrow zigzag stitch, sew around the edges of the applique shapes.

Using two strands of embroidery floss, make two French knots for the cat's eyes and bird's eyes. Backstitch kitten's eyes and bird's legs.

Sew button eye and nose onto the puppy.

Baste piping around perimeter of pillow front. Use a ¼" seam allowance and a zipper foot.

Right sides together, line up the pillow back to the pillow front. Pin in place. Sew around the perimeter of the pillow leaving about a 4" opening at the bottom for turning and stuffing.

Turn pillow right side out. Press. Stuff well with polyester fiberfill. Whipstitch opening closed.

Supplies and Cutting

- A – two 18" x 12 ½" cotton fabric rectangles, one for the pillow front and one for the back
- B – two 18" x 12 ½" rectangles of light fusible interfacing or stabilizer
- Scraps for the applique design shapes.
- Fusible webbing
- 68" of ⅜" wide piping
- ⅛" black button for puppy eye
- ¼" black button for puppy nose
- Dark gray embroidery floss
- Polyester fiberfill

READ

— Tablet Cover —
(iPad case)

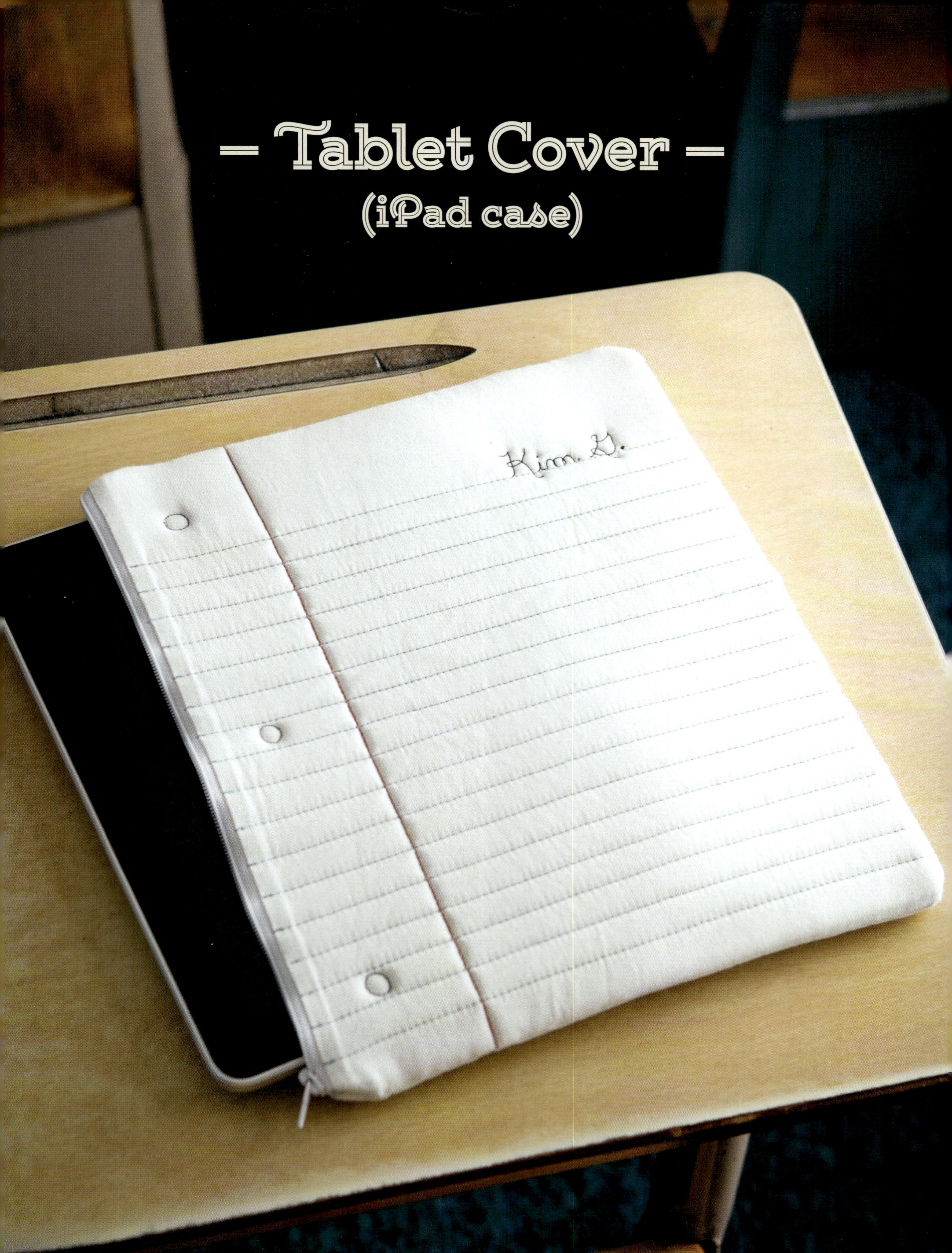

– Tablet Cover –

(iPad case)

Finished size: to fit your device*

Supplies and cutting

- Supplies and cutting
- A – four 12" x 10" rectangles of cotton fabric, two for the case cover, two for the lining
- B – two 11 ½" x 9 ½" rectangles of thin foam
- 12" zipper

Instructions

Right sides together, match up a lining piece A with a cover piece A. Slip the zipper in between these pieces, along the 12" side. Using a ¼" seam allowance and a zipper foot, sew the zipper in place between the layers. Open the fabric away from the zipper and press into place. Repeat the process for the other side of the zipper. *Note: make sure you position the fabric for this step so that the cover fabric is on top of the front side of the zipper.*

Before quilting, slip a foam piece between the cover and the lining on each side of the zipper. Pin or baste in place and quilt.

Finish the case. Right sides together, match the case cover pieces and use a ¼" seam allowance to sew down one side of the case, across the bottom and up the other side. Zigzag stitch around the edge to finish raw seams.

Turn case right side out. Press.

*Modify this pattern for any electronic device. Measure the width and height of your device. Add 2" to the dimensions to get your cutting measurements. For example my iPad measured 10" x 8" so I added 2" to these dimensions and cut pieces that measure 12" x 10". Add 1 ½" to the original dimensions to calculate the cutting dimensions for the foam inserts.

Notebook paper cover: Use the diagram on p. 39 as a guide to quilt the device case to look like a piece of notebook paper. You can even machine embroider your name at the top of the page.

Pieced cover: Piece the front cover in any manner you choose. The one shown to the left was made with old scraps from a Layer Cake. I randomly pieced some leftover 10" wide scrap strips, then trimmed each piece to 10" x 12".

Quilt the first blue line 2 ½″ below the top edge

Space blue lines ½″ apart

Quilt pink line 2¼″ to the right of the left edge. Quilt a second pink line on top of the first to make a bolder line.

Quilt ¼″ circles in dark gray

Kim G.

— Pencil Case —

Pencil Case

Finished size: 6 ½" x 3"

Supplies and cutting

- A - two 7" x 2 ¾" rectangles for pencil case flap front and back
- B – one 6 ½" x 2 ¼" rectangle of medium weight fusible interfacing
- C - two 7 ½" x 2 ¾" rectangles for pencil case pocket
- D – one 7" x 2 ¼" rectangle of medium weight fusible interfacing
- E – two 7 ½ “x 8 ¼" rectangles for pencil case and pencil case lining
- E – one 7 ½" x 8 ¼" rectangle of batting
- F – two 7" x 3" rectangles of medium weight fusible interfacing
- G – one 7" x 1 ¾" rectangle medium weight fusible interfacing
- H – four 9 ½" x 1 ¼" rectangles for zipper sides
- I – two 9" x ¾" rectangles of batting
- J – four 2 ½" x 2 ¼" rectangles for pencil bag sides
- K – two 2" x 1 ¾" rectangles of batting
- 5 ¼" long double fold bias tape
- 9 ½" zipper
- Fabric scraps for flap applique if desired

Instructions

Pencil case flap. Applique the design onto the pencil case flap, piece A, if desired. The templates are on p. 78.

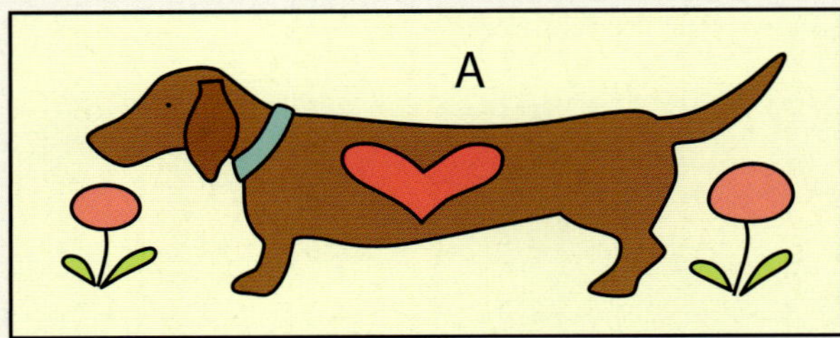

Center the interfacing (piece B) on the wrong side of the flap front, piece A, and fuse.

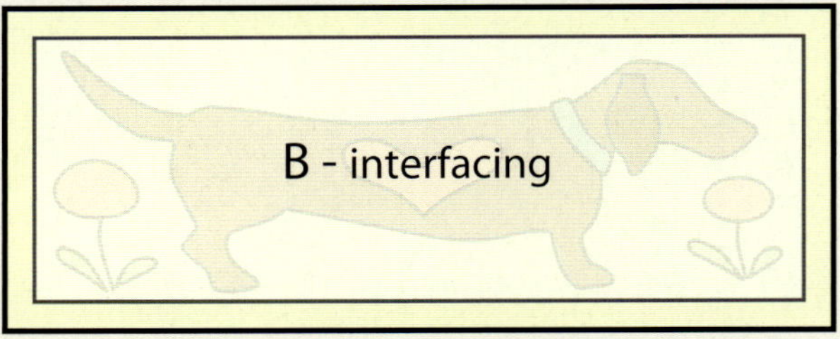

Place the other piece A right sides together with the appliqued piece A. Using a ¼" seam allowance, sew around both sides and bottom of the pencil flap.

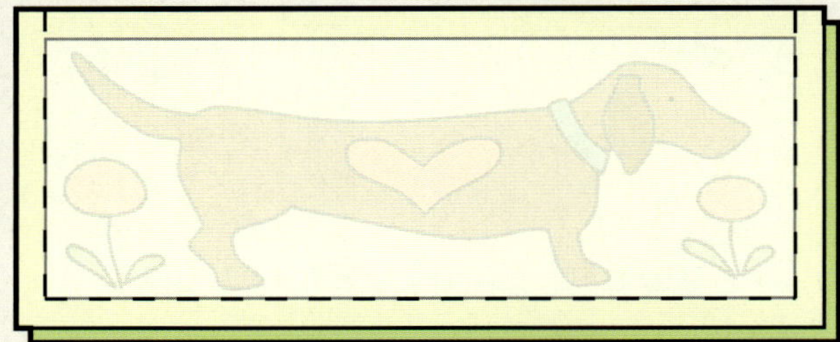

Clip corners, turn and press.

Prepare pocket. Center interfacing piece D on the wrong side of one pocket piece, C.

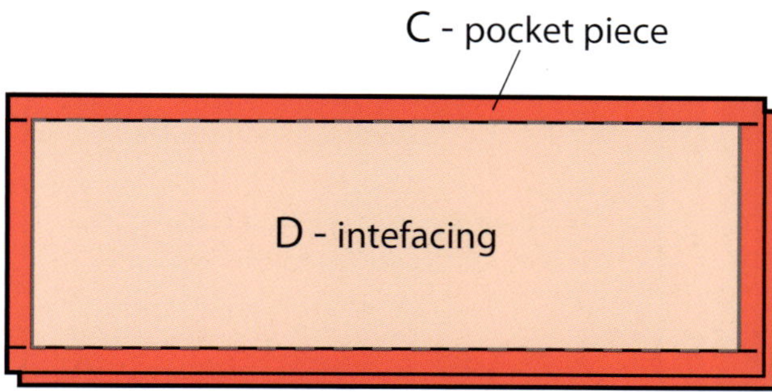

Fuse. Place pocket pieces, C, right sides together. Using a ¼" seam allowance, sew along each of the 7 ½" edges. Turn right side out and press.

Prepare pencil case body. Lay pencil case lining, piece E, wrong side up. Leaving ¼" of space around the perimeter for the seam allowances, lay out the following pieces onto the lining: one piece F, one piece G, then one piece F. Fuse in place.

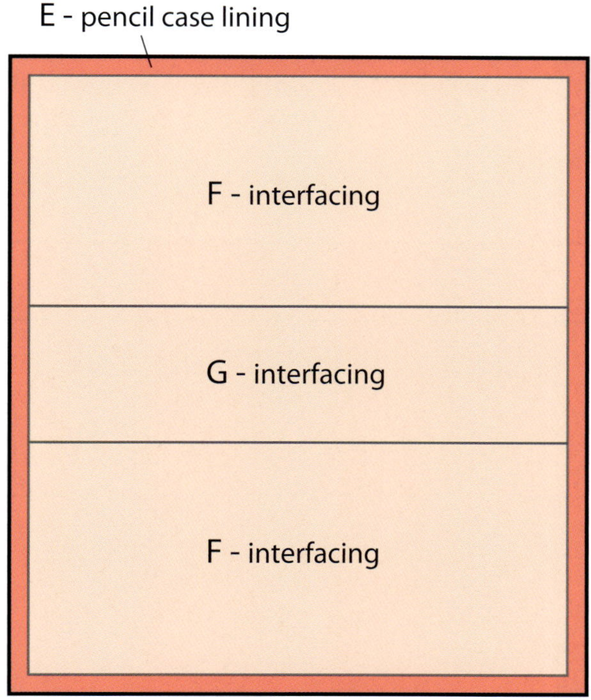

Place the 7 ½ " x 8 ¼" batting, piece E, on top of the lining. Next place the other pencil case piece E on top of the batting, right side up. Press and pin or baste around the edges to hold all pieces together.

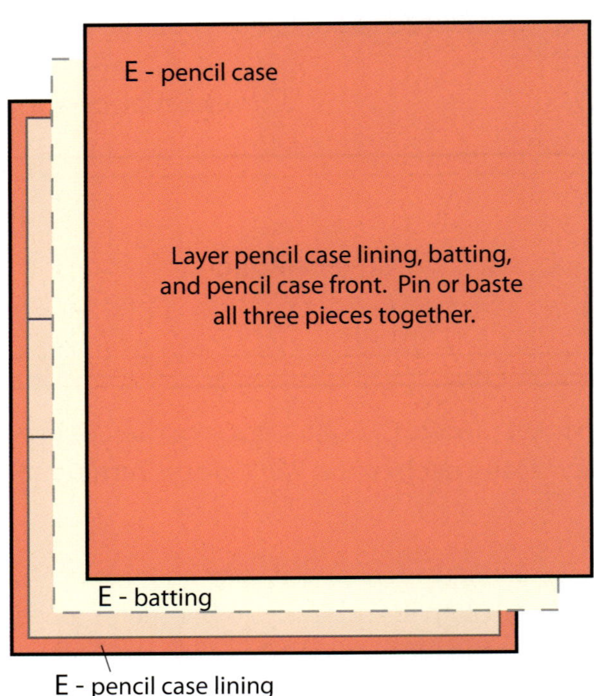

Sew the pocket in place. The top of the pocket should lie 1" below the raw edge of piece E unit. The bottom of the pocket should lie about 3 ¼" from the top so that it kind of matches up with the interfacing piece F.

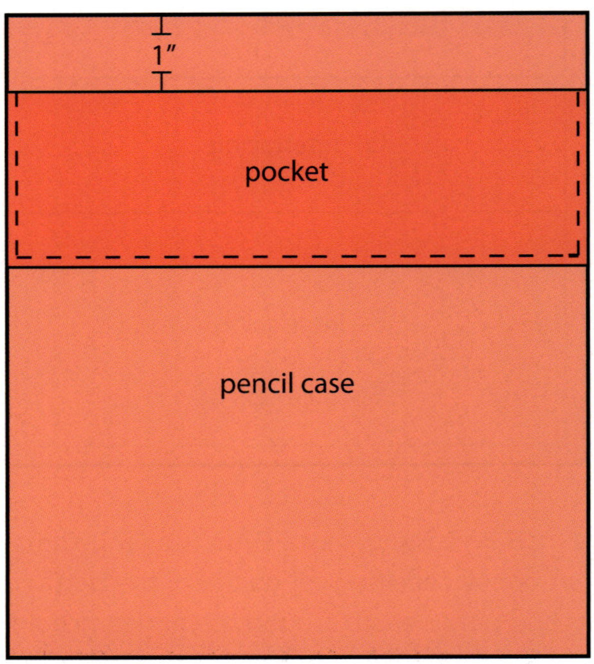

Baste the pencil case flap to the top of this unit.

Sew zipper unit. Take two H pieces (the zipper sides), and place them right sides together.

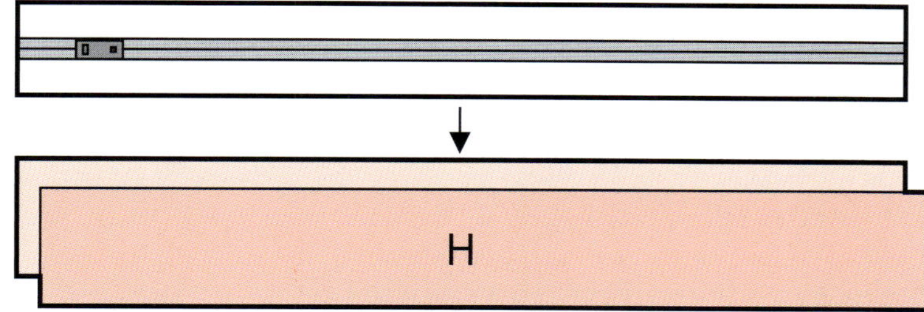

Slip the zipper in between the H zipper sides, and sew, using a ¼" seam allowance and a zipper foot.

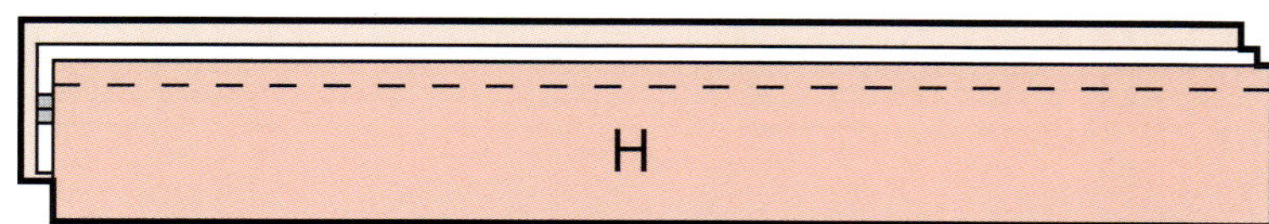

Press sides away from the zipper.

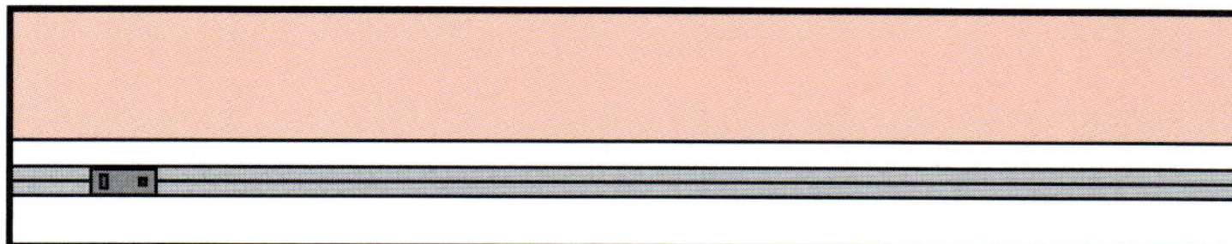

Do the same for the opposite side of the zipper.

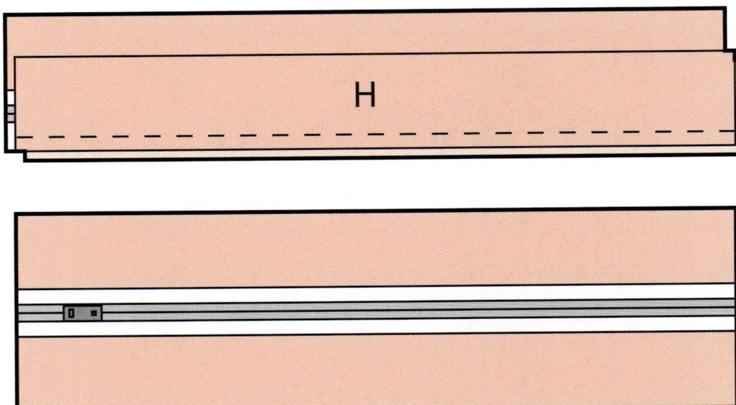

Slip a piece of batting, piece I, in between each zipper side.

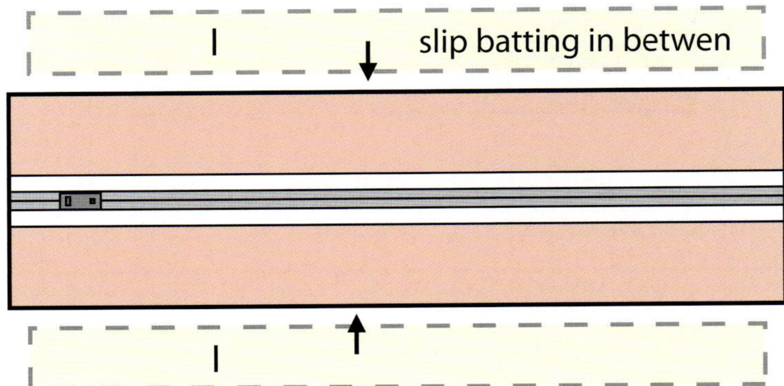

Trim this unit to a 2 ¼" width.

Baste loops to ends of zipper: Cut the bias tape into two 2 ½" long pieces. Fold in the middle and baste to the right sides of the zipper, aligning the loops with the zipper teeth.

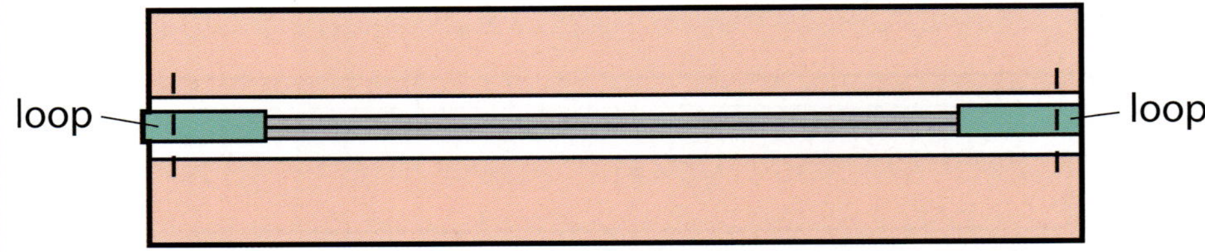

Sew the pencil bag sides to the zipper unit: Take two pencil bag side pieces, piece J, and place them right sides together. Slip one end of the zipper unit in between the two piece J's so that the 2 ¼" edges match. Sew along the 2¼" edge using a ¼" seam allowance. Repeat, sewing to the opposite end.

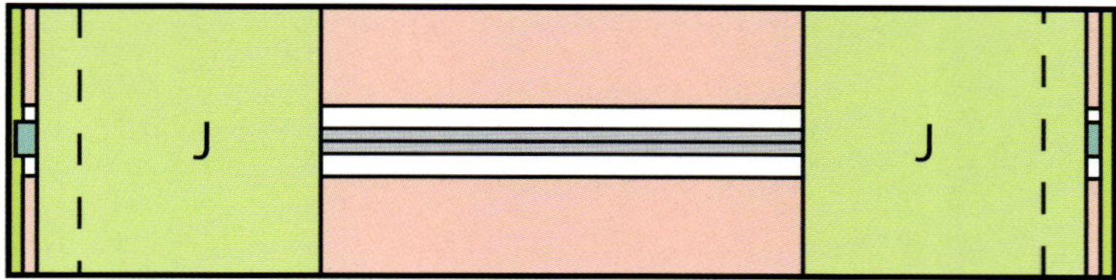

Turn piece J's away from the zipper. Press. Slip in a piece of batting, piece K, in between the piece J's. Hold in place by sewing a line ¼" away from the seam.

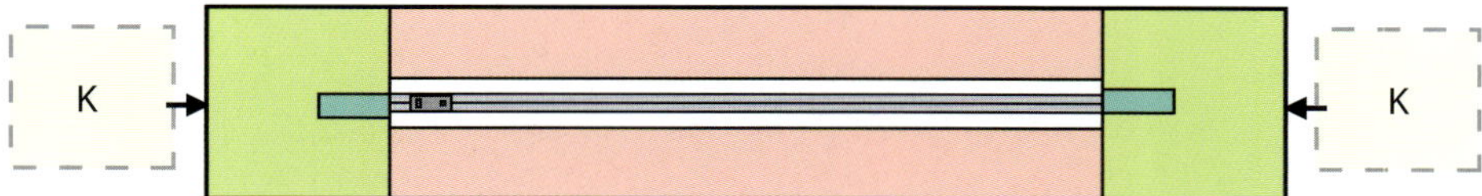

Sew zipper unit to pencil case as follows: Clip what will become the corners of the pencil case. Make scant ¼" clips where the 3" wide and 1 ¾" wide interfacing pieces join up on the pencil case body. Mark where the ¼" seam allowances meet on the wrong side of the zipper unit. This will help you know where to start and stop sewing. Now, right sides together, match the marks on the 2 ¼" edge of the zipper unit with the 1 ¾" wide piece of interfacing of the pencil case. Using a ¼" seam allowance, sew the 2 ¼" edges of the zipper unit to the pencil case body, starting and stopping at the marks. Open the zipper. Sew one side of the zipper unit to the remaining part of the pencil case, and then sew the other side.

Turn the pencil case right side out through the open zipper.

– Reusable Sandwich Bag –

Finished size: 7 ½" x 6 ½"

Instructions

Applique the front of the sandwich bag if desired. See instructions on page 5.

Prepare the zipper. The final zipper will measure 8" long and have a ¾" stay at each end so that the zipper opening is 6½". Mark an 8" segment of the zipper.

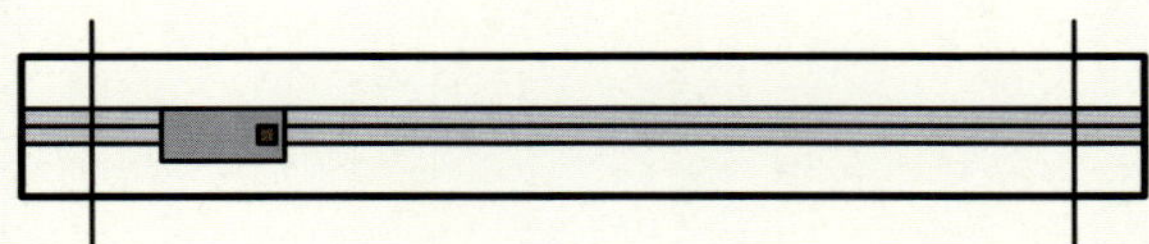

Now mark lines ½" inside of the first lines. Sandwich the bottom end of the zipper in between two of the 1" square zipper stops (right sides together). The zipper stop squares should line up with the second marked line and the squares should be directed towards the middle of the zipper. Sew a seam ¼" away from the marked line.

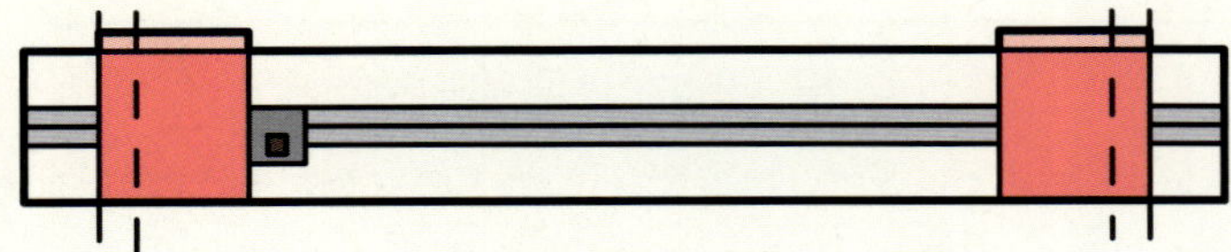

Press the zipper stop squares away from the center of the zipper.

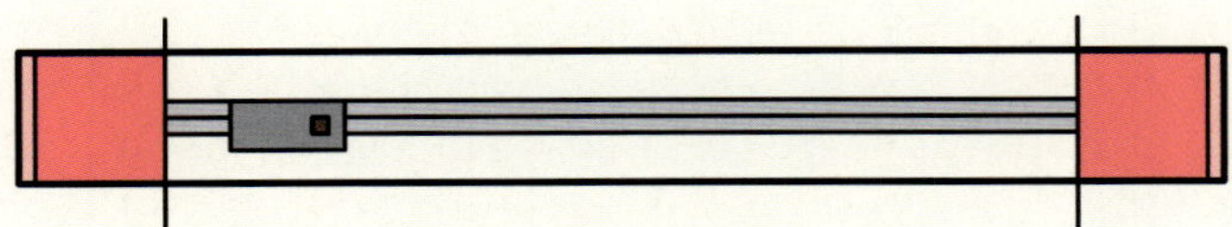

Trim the zipper ¼" away from the sewn line. Open the zipper so that the zipper pull is inside the 8" line, and then sew the zipper stop on the top end of the zipper in the same manner as the bottom zipper stop.

Sew the zipper to the bag pieces. Lay the sandwich bag front on a table right side up with the 8" side at the top. Lay the zipper, right

Supplies and cutting

- Two 8" x 7" rectangles of cotton fabric for front and back
- Two 8" x 7" rectangles of fabric or food-safe vinyl for lining
- Three 8" x 1½" rectangles for binding
- Four 1" squares for zipper stops
- Cotton scraps for applique design (optional)
- Two 7" x 6" rectangles of thin foam or batting
- One 9" zipper
- Fusible webbing (optional)

side down, on the 8" bag top. The zipper pull should be on the left side. Now lay one lining piece on top of the zipper, right side down.

Put a zipper foot on your sewing machine and sew along the 8" top edge through all three layers. Open and press. Sew the back and other lining piece to the other side of the zipper in the same manner.

Add foam or batting. Insert a piece of foam in between the front and lining, and the back and lining. There should be at least ¼" free space along all raw edges.

Sew bag. Fold bag over so that the lining pieces lay right sides together as in a finished bag. Use a ¼" seam allowance to sew around the remaining three edges.

Finish the sandwich bag's raw edges with the 8" x 1½" rectangles. Start by binding the bottom edge. Right sides together, sew a long strip to the bottom, using a seam allowance just a little wider than ¼" to hide the primary stitching. Press under a scant ¼" seam allowance along the remaining 8" edge of the binding fabric. Fold the binding over the sandwich bag and press. Either whipstitch the binding down or machine stitch. Now bind the side pieces. Sew in a like manner but first fold over each short edge by ½" so there will be no raw edges when finished.

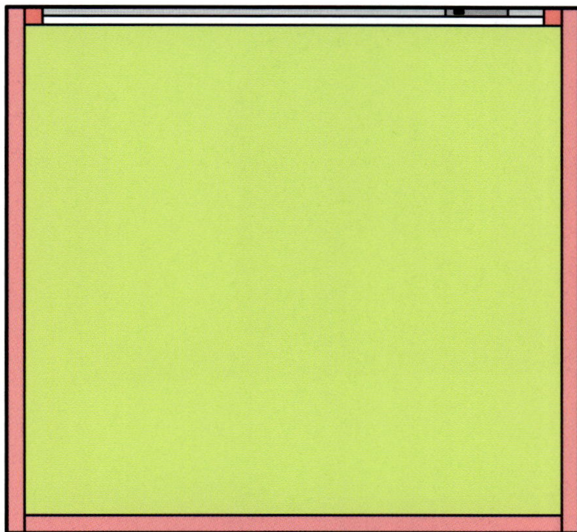

Matthew

— Lunch Bag —

Finished size: 7 ½" x 9" x 4"

Instructions

Quilt each lunch bag component: You will need two quilted A units for lunch bag front and back, two quilted B units for lunch bag sides, and one C unit for lunch bag bottom. To make a unit, sandwich a foam or batting piece inside a lining piece and a lunch bag piece. Baste and quilt as desired. I used a 2" diagonal pattern.

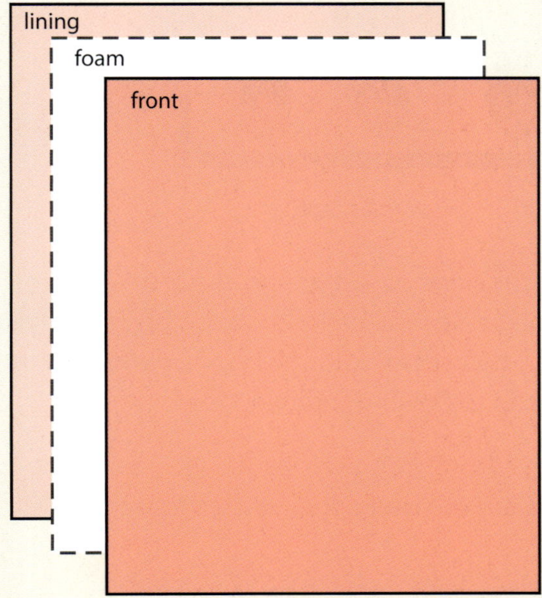

Piece and quilt lunch bag top flap. Use ¼" seam allowances. For the strawberry lunch bag, applique the strawberries onto piece F, then sew piece E to the top of piece F.

Supplies and cutting

- A - two 8" x 9 ½" rectangles for bag front and back
- A - two 8" x 9 ½" rectangles for bag lining
- A - two 8" x 9 ½" rectangles of foam or batting
- B - two 4 ½" x 9 ½" rectangles for bag sides
- B - two 4 ½" x 9 ½" rectangles for bag lining
- B - two 4 ½" x 9 ½" rectangles of foam or batting
- C - one 8" x 4 ½" rectangle for bottom
- C - one 8" x 4 ½" rectangle for bottom lining
- C - one 8" x 4 ½" rectangle of foam or batting
- D - one 7 ½" x 4 ½" rectangle for top flap lining
- D - one 7 ½" x 4 ½" rectangle of foam or batting
- 5" length of hook and loop tape
- 9 ½" length of 1" wide strap or belting for handle
- 40" of ¼" wide double fold bias tape

For strawberry lunch bag:

(The strawberry template is on p. 79)

- E - 7 ½" x 2 ½" white fabric, applique strawberries on this piece before sewing
- F - 7 ½" x 2 ½" green

For spaceship lunch bag:

- E – 7 ½" x 2 ½" gray fabric
- G – 7 ½" x 1 ¼" gray fabric
- H – 7 ½" x 1 ¾" yellow fabric, embroider name on this piece before sewing

For the spaceship bag, embroider a name onto piece H then sew pieces E and G to the unit to complete the top.

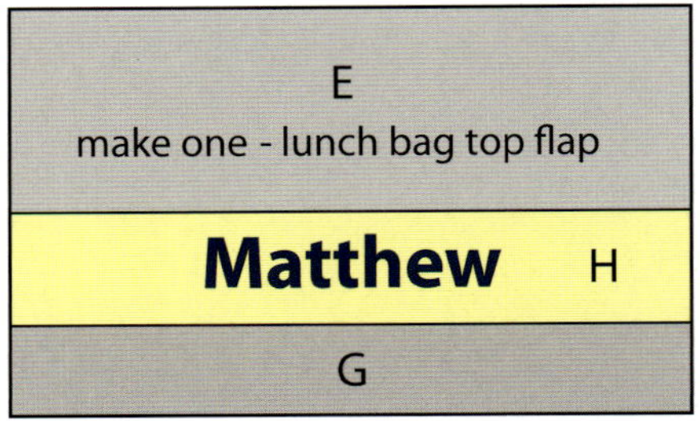

Add foam and lining, then quilt as desired. Finally finish the side and bottom edge of the lunch bag flap with bias tape.

Construct bag body. Right sides together and using a ¼" seam allowance, sew lunch bag sides (piece B), to lunch bag front (piece A) along the 9 ½" edge. Then sew the lunch bag back to the side pieces. Use a zigzag stitch to finish the raw edges.

Right sides together, sew lunch bag bottom, piece C, to the body of the constructed bag. Finish the raw edges with a zigzag stitch. Turn right side out.

Attach strap and flap: Baste each end of the lunch bag handle to the lunch bag back, ¾" away from the side seam.

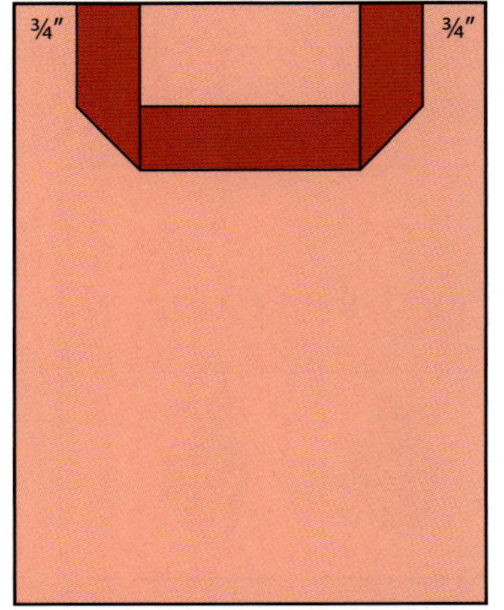

Right sides together and using a ¼" seam allowance, sew the lunch bag flap to the bag back. The bag handle ends will be caught in this seam.

Finish the raw edge of the lunch bag opening with double-folded bias tape.

Hand stitch hook and loop tape to the front of the bag and the underside of the lunch bag flap.

— Lunch Purse (view A) —

Finished size: 12" x 10 ½" x 3"

Supplies and cutting

- A - two 12 ½" x 7 ½" rectangles for purse front and back (top)
- B – two 12 ½" x 5 ½" rectangles for purse front and back (bottom)
- C - two 12 ½" squares lining fabric
- D - two 12" square pieces of thin foam or batting
- E - four 12 ½" x 1 ½" rectangles for zipper inset
- F – two 12" x 1" rectangles batting for zipper inset
- G – four 1" squares for zipper stops
- H - four 18" x 2" strips of fabric for purse handles
- I - two 16" x 1" strips of medium weight interfacing for purse handles
- One 12 ½" zipper

Instructions

Right sides together, and using a ¼" seam allowance, sew each purse piece A (top) to purse piece B (bottom) along the 12 ½" edge. Press seam open. These are the front and back pieces for your purse.

Cut a 2" square from the right and left bottom corners of purse front and back pieces and from the bag linings, piece C.

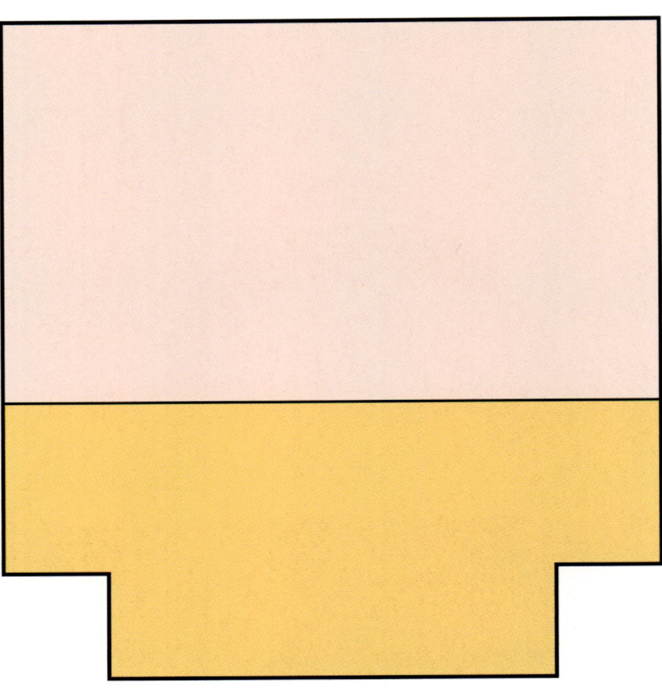

Cut a 2 ¼" square out of the right and left bottom corners of both foam pieces, piece D.

Make a "quilt sandwich" for the purse front and back, by centering each piece of foam (piece D) in between a piece A/B and a lining piece C. The wrong sides of the A/B piece and purse lining should be facing the foam. Baste or pin the quilt sandwich in place, then machine quilt. I used a 2" diagonal grid pattern to quilt the model. If you're having problems getting all three layers of fabric and foam to feed through your sewing machine evenly, try sewing with a walking foot attachment so the top layer of fabric will feed through at the same time the bottom layer of fabric does.

Once the purse front and back pieces are quilted, stabilize the raw edges by sewing around the perimeter of each piece using a ⅛" seam allowance.

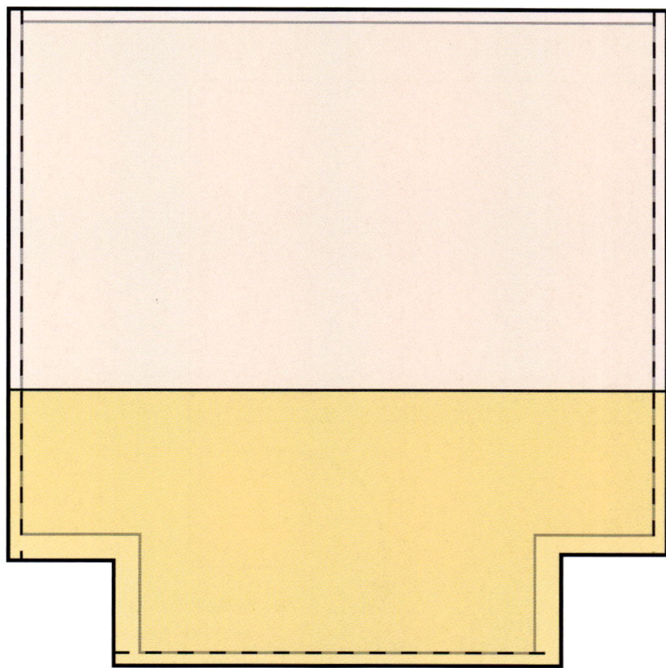

You should be sewing only through the fabric and not the foam.

Now you're ready to sew the front and back purse pieces together. Right sides together, match the purse front and back. Use a ¼" seam allowance to sew a seam down each side, and then across the bottom of the purse. Use a zigzag stitch to finish off the raw edges of the two sides and bottom. Don't turn this unit right side out yet.

In this step you will sew a gusset at each bottom corner of the purse. This will give the purse a flat bottom and allow it to stand on its own. With right sides together, fold one of the purse's side seams down to meet the bottom seam.

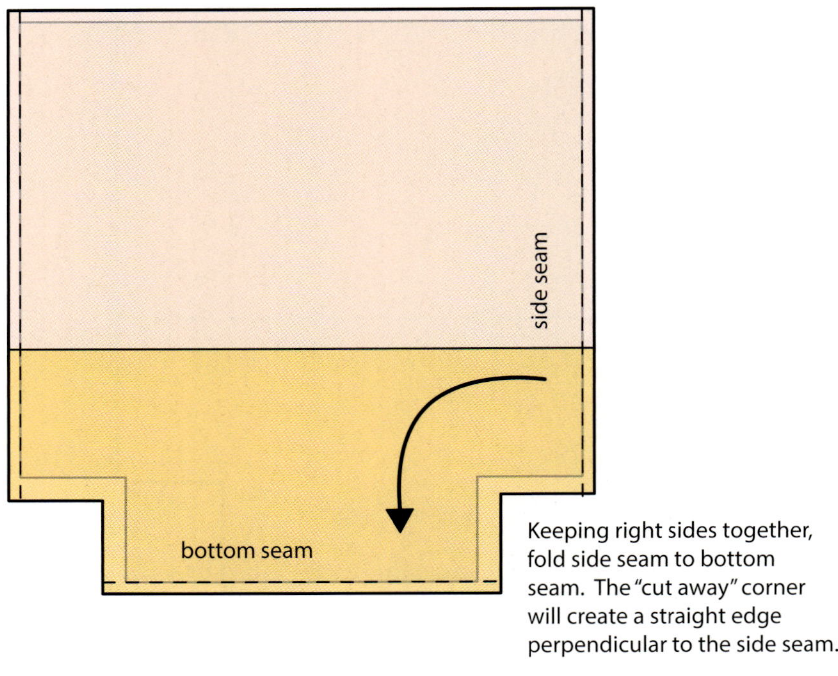

Match up the seams at the bottom of the purse. The corner cut-out should now form a straight line at a 90 degree angle to the purse side seam. Sew along this line using a ¼" seam allowance.

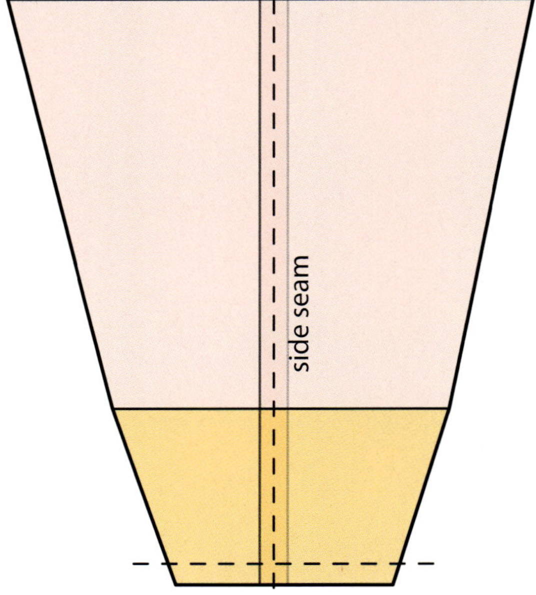

Repeat this process for the opposite corner. Finish the seams with a zigzag stitch to prevent the fabric from unraveling.

Finish the zipper ends. Lay the two square zipper stop pieces, piece G, right sides together. Slip one end of the zipper in between the two G pieces. Using a ½" seam allowance (note that it's wide, a one-half inch seam allowance), sew through the zipper stops and zipper.

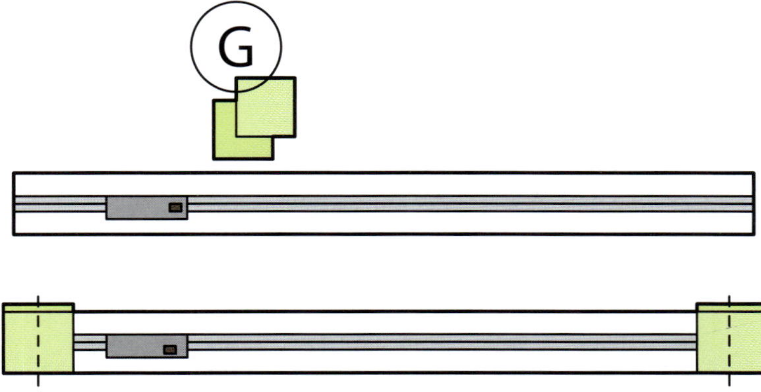

Do the same for the opposite end of the zipper. Press the zipper stop pieces back away from the center of the zipper. Trim the seam allowance and extra zipper fabric. The zipper with zipper stops should still measure 12 ½".

Construct the zipper unit. Right sides together, match up two zipper inset pieces, piece E. Slip the zipper into the center of the two E pieces, matching the 12 ½" sides.

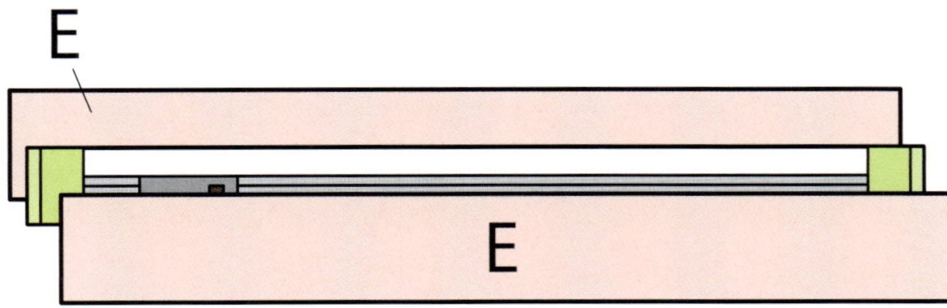

Use a zipper foot on your sewing machine to sew along the 12 ½" side using a ¼" seam allowance. Press zipper inset pieces back away from the zipper.

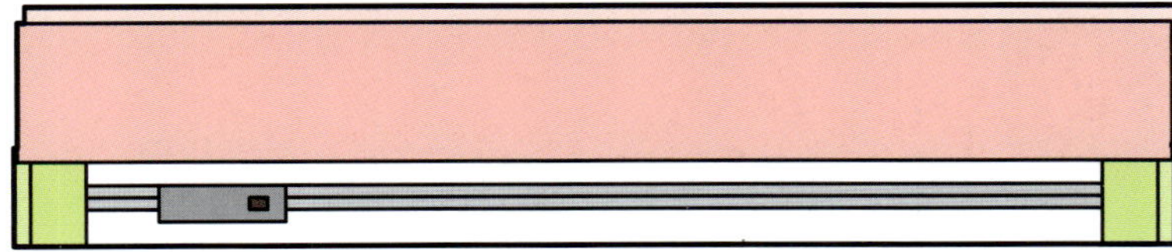

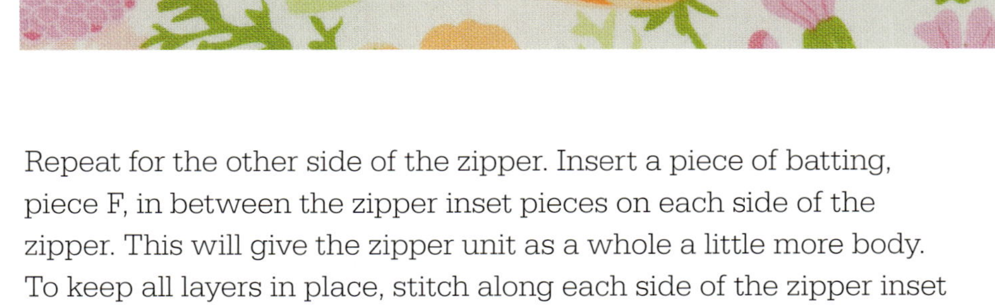

Repeat for the other side of the zipper. Insert a piece of batting, piece F, in between the zipper inset pieces on each side of the zipper. This will give the zipper unit as a whole a little more body. To keep all layers in place, stitch along each side of the zipper inset piece about ⅛" from where the zipper inset piece meets the zipper body. Also stitch the raw edges together using a ⅛" seam allowance. Fold the zipper in the middle along the zipper teeth, right sides together.

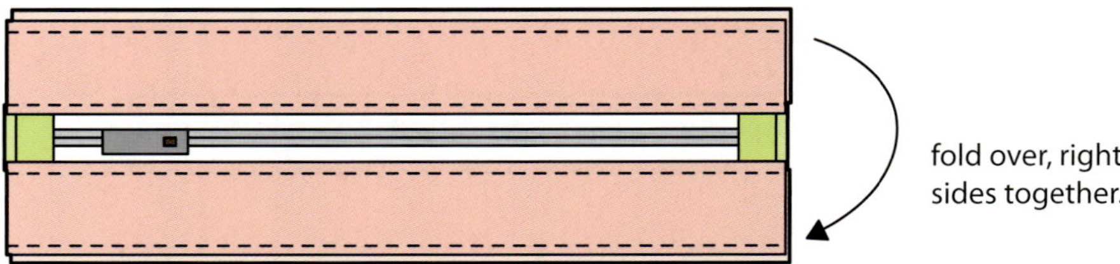

Use a ¼" seam allowance to sew across the 1 ½" edges.

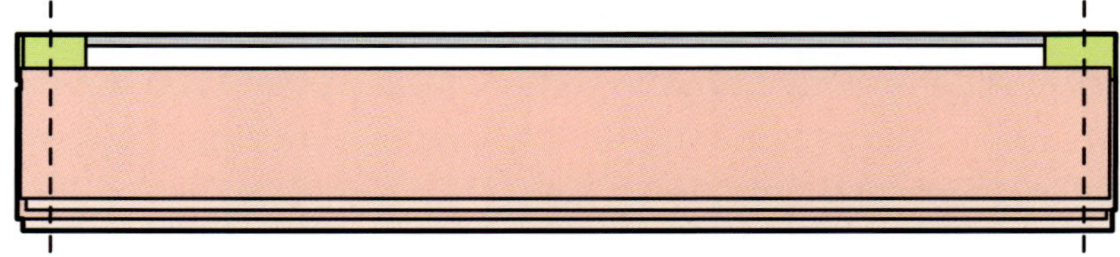

Attach the zipper unit. Start by making sure the purse and zipper units are wrong side out. Open the zipper all the way. Matching the side seams, pin the zipper unit to the opening of the purse, right sides together. Sew around the purse opening using a ¼" seam allowance. Zigzag the raw edges to finish. Turn the purse right side out. Iron the top seam so that the zipper section is recessed into the purse body. Reinforce by stitching around the top edge of the purse ⅛" away from the top seam.

Sew the purse handles. Center an interfacing piece I on the wrong side of a purse handle, piece H. If the interfacing is fusible, make sure the fusible side is facing the wrong side of the fabric. Fuse in place (optional). Turn the raw edges over the interfacing along the 18" side and press well. Repeat with one more piece H and the remaining piece I. These are the purse handles. Now take the other two purse handle pieces, piece H, and press ½" seams along each long edge. These are the purse handle facing. With the turned under edges of both pieces hidden in the center, match each purse handle with a purse handle facing. Sew along each long side about 3/16" from the edge. Turn under each raw end about 1". The fabric should turn well because the interfacing is about 1" shorter than the purse handle. Press.

Use the diagram to align purse handles to purse. Pin in place and sew to the purse. Make sure the zipper unit is maneuvered so that it does not get caught in the seam.

Finishing touch – If your zipper pull feels small, thread a few inches of grosgrain ribbon through the hole in the zipper pull and tie. Clip the edges of the ribbon for a pretty effect.

— Lunch Purse (view B) —

Finished size: 12" x 10 ½" x 3"

Supplies and cutting:

- A - two 12 ½" x 7" rectangles for purse front and back (top)
- B – Cut between eight to 16 – 12 ½" long strips of green and brown fabrics that vary in width from 1" to 1 ½". Piece the strips along the long edge to create two 12 ½" x 6" rectangles for purse front and back (bottom).
- C - two 12 ½" squares lining fabric
- D - two 12" square pieces of thin foam or batting
- E - four 12 ½" x 1 ½" rectangles for zipper inset
- F – two 12" x 1" rectangles batting for zipper inset
- G - four 1" squares for zipper stops
- H - four 18" x 2" strips of fabric for purse handles
- I - two 16" x 1" strips of medium weight interfacing for purse handles
- One 12 ½" zipper

Instructions

Cut all pieces, then applique the floral design onto piece A. Templates are on p. 80. See applique instructions on pg. 5. Use strips of different green and brown fabrics that vary in widths from 1" to 1 ½", to piece the bottom of the purse, piece B. Construct the purse as instructions above indicate. Modify quilting as appropriate to design. I stitched in the ditch in between the green and brown strips, and then stippled in between the applique flower designs. Sew buttons in the center of the flowers and add embroidered details after you quilt, but before you construct the purse.

Templates

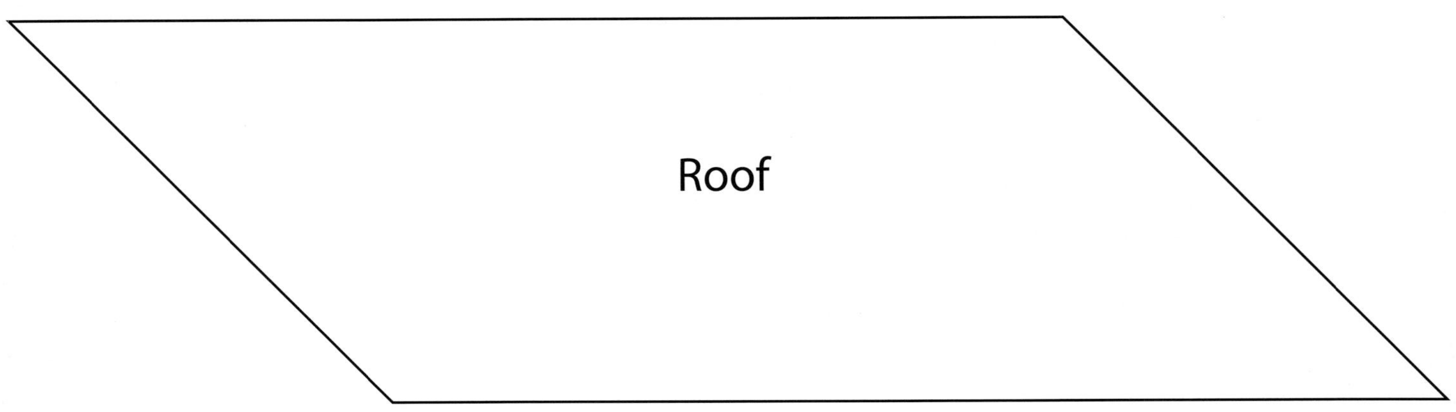

Schoolhouse

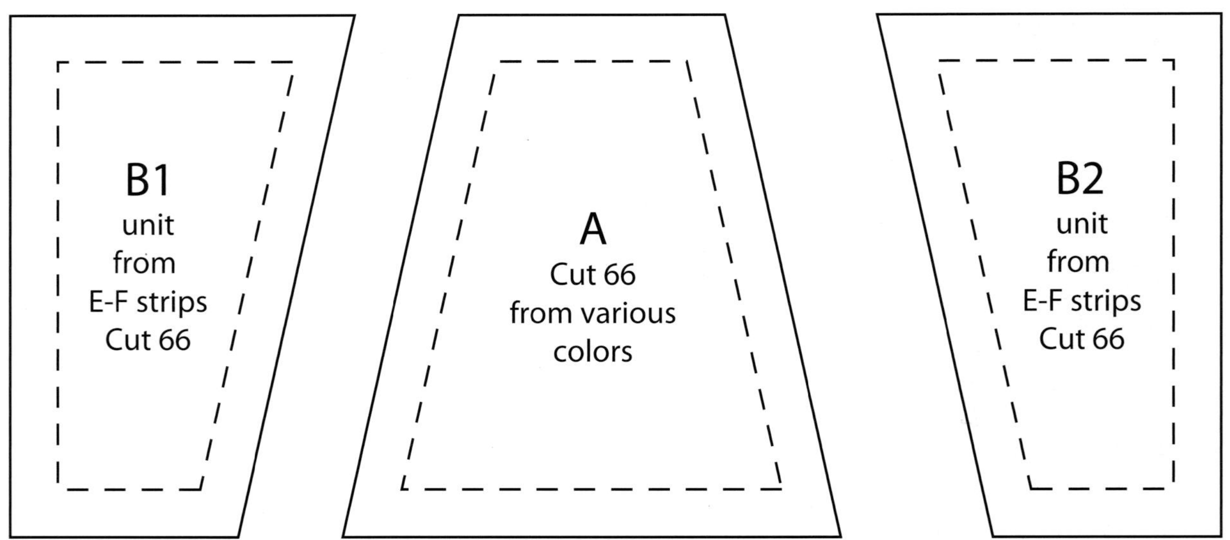

Kids

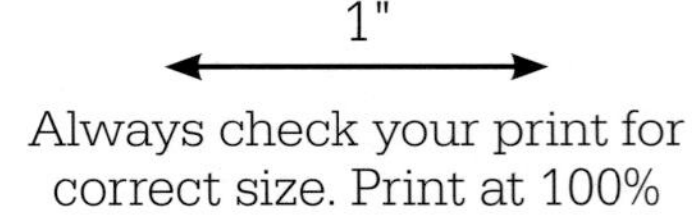

Always check your print for correct size. Print at 100%

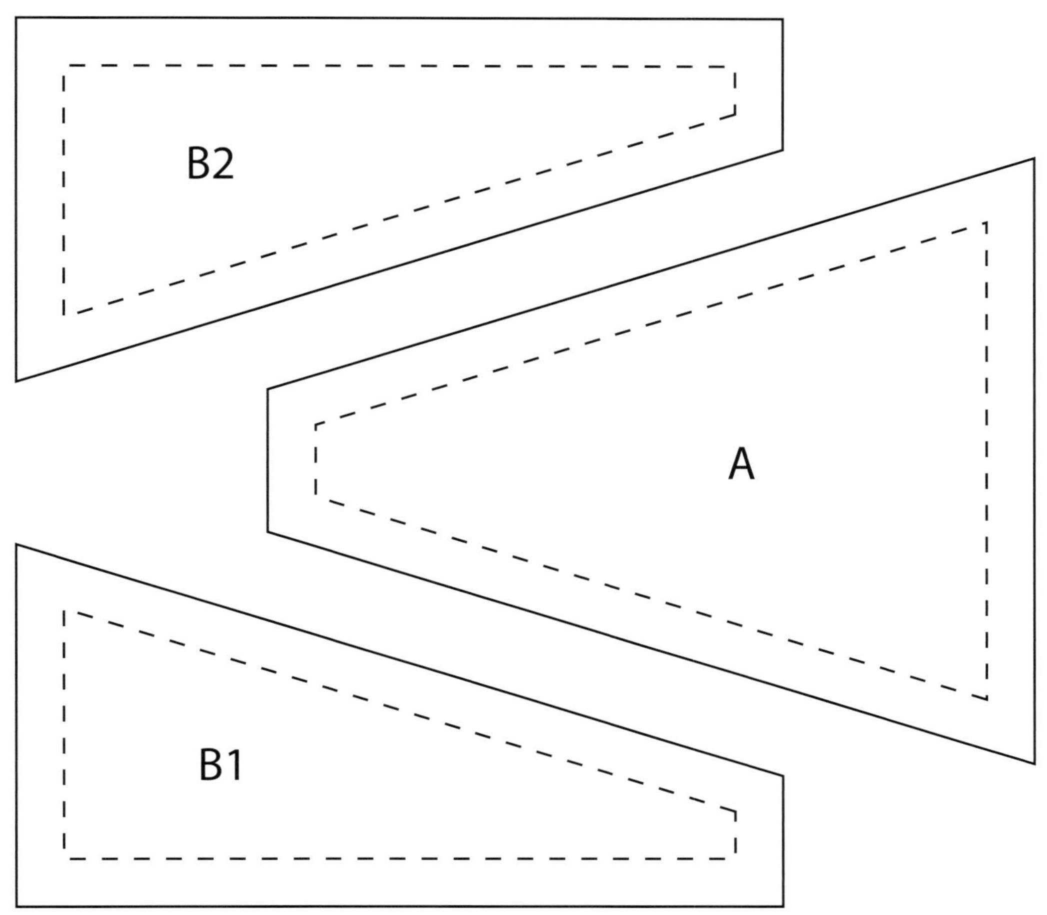

Pencils and Crayons

Crayon point, cut 40 total from various colors

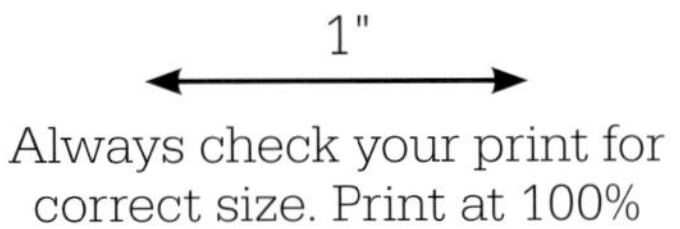

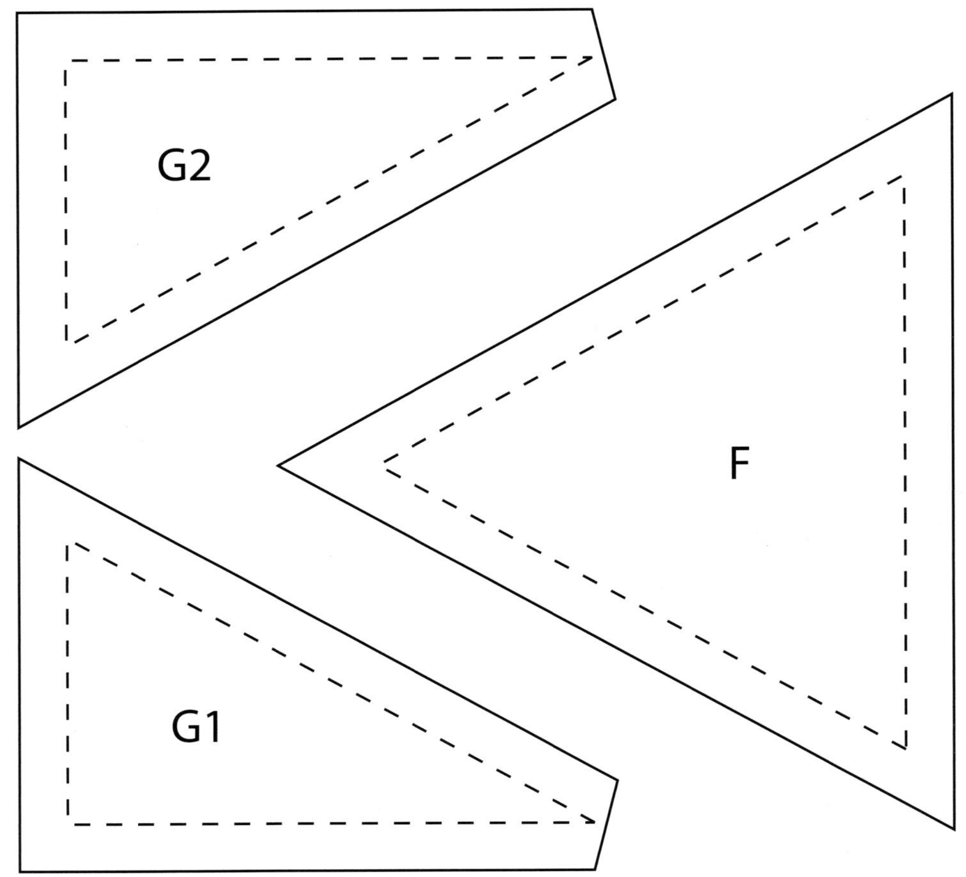

Pencils and Crayons

Pencil point, cut 14 from pieced strip

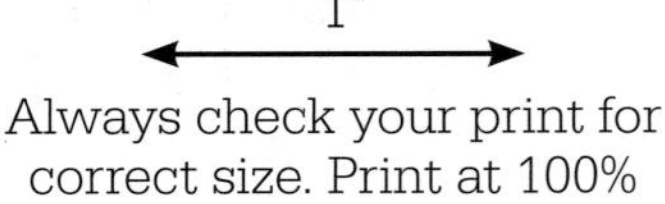

1"

Always check your print for correct size. Print at 100%

Reading Pillow

Reading Pillow

1"

Always check your print for correct size. Print at 100%

Reading Pillow

1"

Always check your print for correct size. Print at 100%

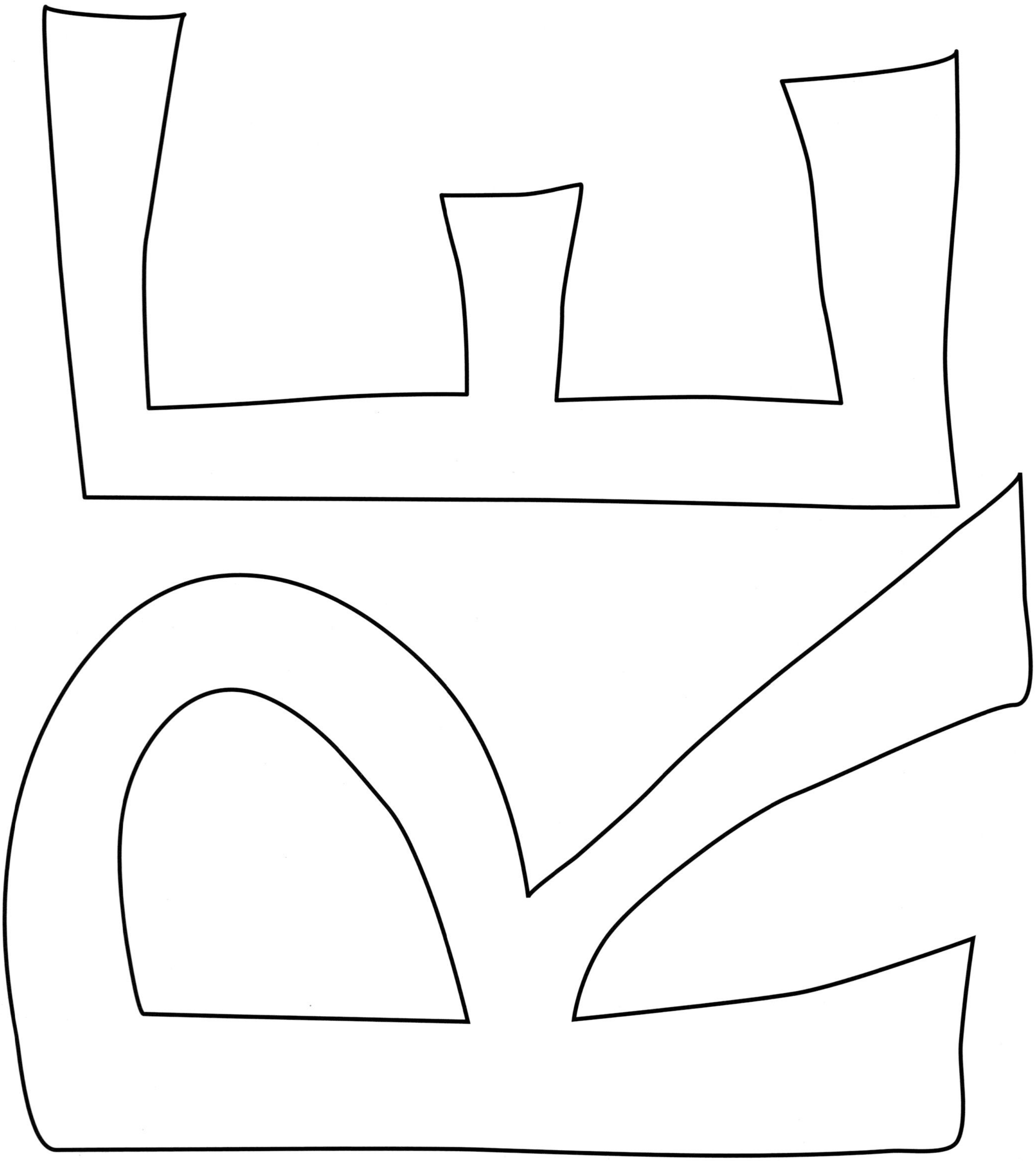

Reading Pillow

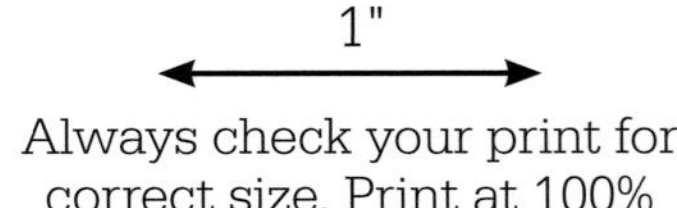

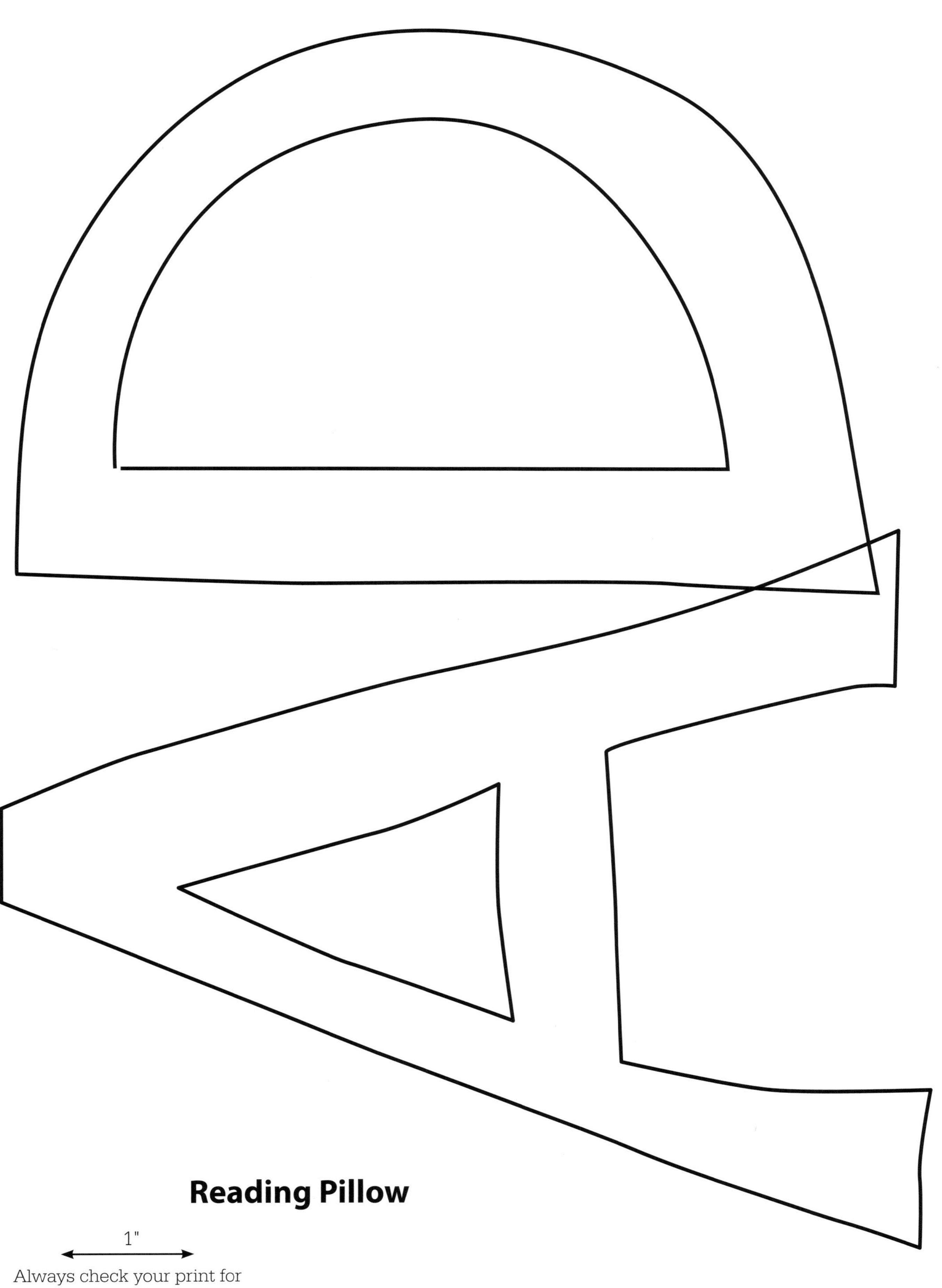

Reading Pillow

1"

Always check your print for correct size. Print at 100%

Pencil Case

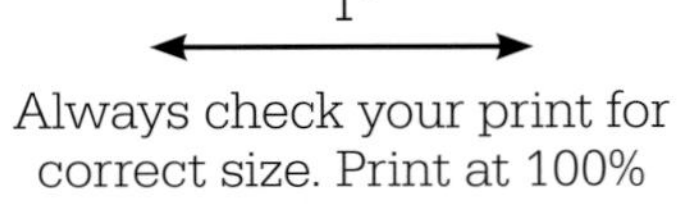

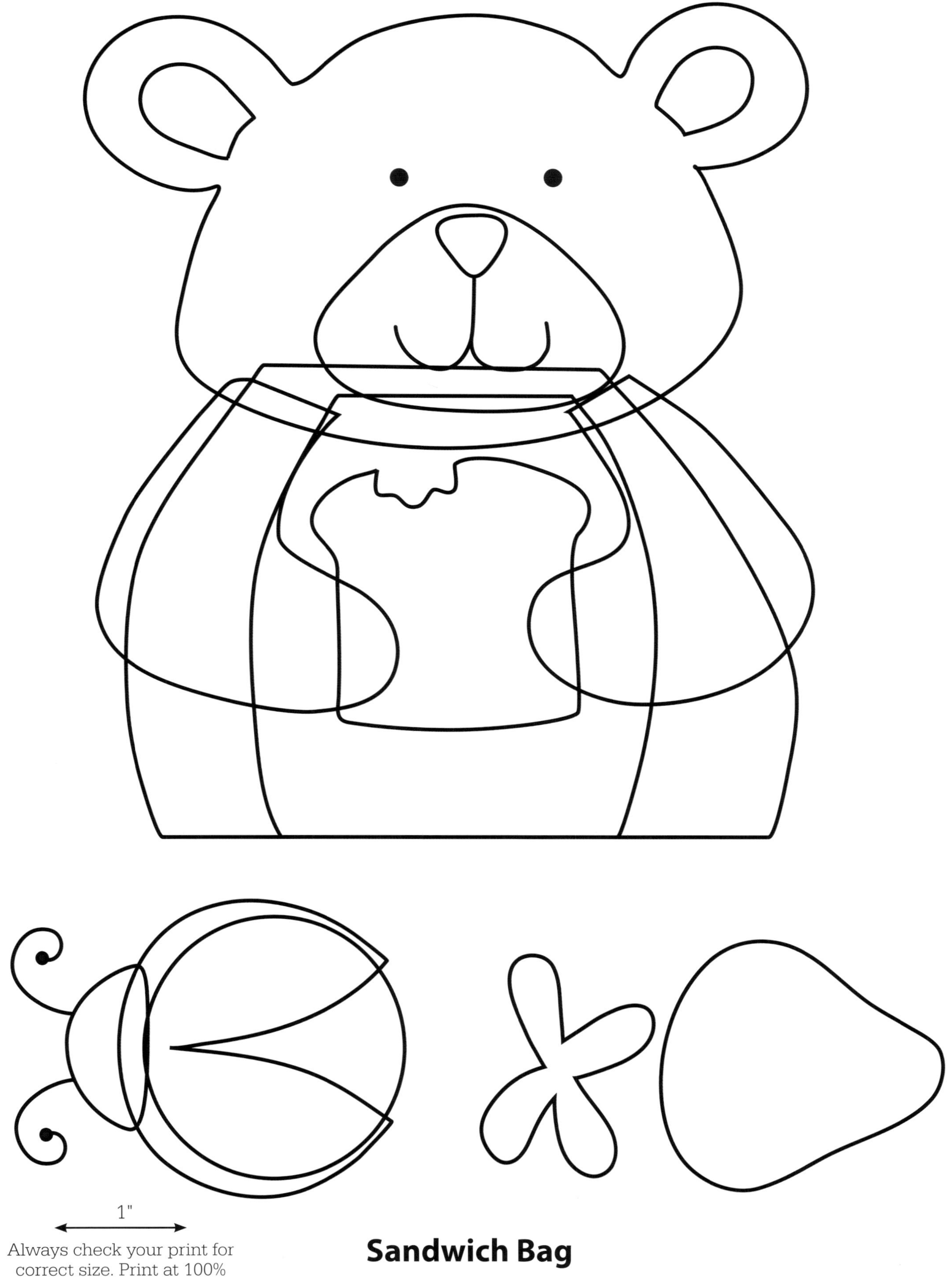

Sandwich Bag

1"

Always check your print for correct size. Print at 100%

Lunch Purse